NATIVE AMERICANS: RIGHTS, LAWS AND LEGISLATIVE DEVELOPMENTS

NATIVE AMERICANS: RIGHTS, LAWS AND LEGISLATIVE DEVELOPMENTS

CHARLES P. TOWNSEND
EDITOR

Nova Science Publishers, Inc.
New York

Copyright © 2008 by Nova Science Publishers, Inc.

All rights reserved. No part of this book may be reproduced, stored in a retrieval system or transmitted in any form or by any means: electronic, electrostatic, magnetic, tape, mechanical photocopying, recording or otherwise without the written permission of the Publisher.

For permission to use material from this book please contact us:
Telephone 631-231-7269; Fax 631-231-8175
Web Site: http://www.novapublishers.com

NOTICE TO THE READER

The Publisher has taken reasonable care in the preparation of this book, but makes no expressed or implied warranty of any kind and assumes no responsibility for any errors or omissions. No liability is assumed for incidental or consequential damages in connection with or arising out of information contained in this book. The Publisher shall not be liable for any special, consequential, or exemplary damages resulting, in whole or in part, from the readers' use of, or reliance upon, this material.

Independent verification should be sought for any data, advice or recommendations contained in this book. In addition, no responsibility is assumed by the publisher for any injury and/or damage to persons or property arising from any methods, products, instructions, ideas or otherwise contained in this publication.

This publication is designed to provide accurate and authoritative information with regard to the subject matter covered herein. It is sold with the clear understanding that the Publisher is not engaged in rendering legal or any other professional services. If legal or any other expert assistance is required, the services of a competent person should be sought. FROM A DECLARATION OF PARTICIPANTS JOINTLY ADOPTED BY A COMMITTEE OF THE AMERICAN BAR ASSOCIATION AND A COMMITTEE OF PUBLISHERS.

LIBRARY OF CONGRESS CATALOGING-IN-PUBLICATION DATA

Native Americans : rights, laws and legislative developments / Charles P. Townsend, editor.
   p. cm.
   ISBN 978-1-60456-202-6 (hardcover)
   1. Indians of North America--Civil rights. 2. Indians of North America--Legal status, laws, etc. 3. Indians of North America--Politics and government. 4. Legislation--United States. 5. United States--Politics and government. I. Townsend, Charles P.

KF8210.C5A74 2007
342.7308'72--dc22
                        2007045973

Published by Nova Science Publishers, Inc. ✣ *New York*

CONTENTS

Preface		vii
Chapter 1	Indian Health Service: Health Care Delivery, Status, Funding, and Legislative Issues *Donna U. Vogt and Roger Walke*	1
Chapter 2	Indian Reserved Water Rights: An Overview *Nathan Brooks*	51
Chapter 3	Native American Graves Protection and Repatriation Act (NAGPRA): Legal and Legislative Developments *Douglas Reid Weimer*	71
Chapter 4	Indian Self-Determination and Education Assistance Act Contracts and Cherokee Nation of Oklahoma V. Leavitt: Agency Discretion to Fund Contract Support Costs *Nathan Brooks*	89
Chapter 5	Native American Issues in the 109th Congress *Roger Walke*	101
Chapter 6	Child Custody Proceedings under the Indian Child Welfare Act: An Overview *Kamilah M. Holder*	111
Chapter 7	Indian Gaming Regulatory Act: Gaming on Newly Acquired Lands *M. Maureen Murphy*	121

Chapter 8	State Regulation of Tribal Lands in New York: City of Sherrill v. Oneida Indian Nation of New York *Nathan Brooks*	**131**
Chapter 9	The Bureau of Indian Affairs' Process for Recognizing Groups as Indian Tribes *M. Maureen Murphy*	**139**
Chapter 10	Application of Campaign Finance Law to Indian Tribes *L. Paige Whitaker and Joseph E. Cantor*	**147**
Index		**155**

PREFACE

Native American issues continue to constitute an important part of the federal government's responsibility. Native Americans in the United States are the indigenous peoples from the regions of North America now encompassed by the continental United States, including parts of Alaska. They comprise a large number of distinct tribes, states, and ethnic groups, many of which are still enduring as political communities. There is a wide range of terms used, and some controversy surrounding their use: they are variously known as American Indians, Indians, Amerindians, Amerinds, or Indigenous, Aboriginal or Original Americans.There are 561 federally recognized tribal governments in the United States. These tribes possess the right to form their own government, to enforce laws (both civil and criminal), to tax, to establish membership, to license and regulate activities, to zone and to exclude persons from tribal territories. Limitations on tribal powers of self-government include the same limitations applicable to states; for example, neither tribes nor states have the power to make war, engage in foreign relations, or coin money (this includes paper currency).

This new book presents the latest developments in the areas of rights, laws and legislation.

Chapter 1 - The Indian Health Service (IHS), an agency in the Department of Health and Human Services (HHS), funds health care for eligible American Indians/Alaskan Natives (AI/AN) through a system of programs and facilities located on or near Indian reservations and in certain urban areas. The IHS health delivery program is organized in 12 regional area offices and 167 local service units, and serves federal reservations, Indian communities, and urban Indians. In general, persons eligible for IHS services must be in IHS service areas and belong to federally recognized tribes.

The IHS-served population generally has a higher incidence of illness and premature mortality than the general U.S. population. Several annual IHS publications compare the health conditions and causes of death of the IHS service population with those for the general U.S. population. According to the latest of these, the average life expectancy at birth for the IHS service area population in 1996-1998 was 70.6 years, or 5.9 years less than the 76.5 years for the total U.S. 1997 population.

IHS appropriations are separated into two budget categories: health services and health facilities. For FY2006, the appropriations for health services is $2.692 billion and for health facilities $353 million. Of the total appropriation of $3.045 billion, 88% is for health services and 12% for health facilities. Other sources of funding include reimbursements from Medicare, Medicaid, and private insurance. If Indians are eligible and are recipients of such programs, IHS becomes the residual payer or "the payer of last resort." This means that IHS pays only after all other sources of payment have been exhausted.

While a number of legislative issues concerning IHS face the 109th Congress, congressional committees have focused primarily on the reauthorization of the Indian Health Care Improvement Act (IHCIA), which provides specific statutory authority for many IHS programs. Thus far two bills (S. 1057 and H.R. 5312) have been introduced in the 109th Congress to reauthorize the IHCIA, and another bill (S. 3524) has been introduced to amend, or create, IHCIA provisions in the Social Security Act. Both reauthorization bills would increase tribal participation in negotiated rule-making, elevate the position of the Director of IHS within the HHS to the level of Assistant Secretary for Indian Health, expand health services, increase reimbursement options from other federal programs, and authorize other actions. S. 1057 was reported, amended, by the Senate Indian Affairs Committee on March 16 (S.Rept. 109-222), H.R. 5312 was ordered reported, amended, by the House Resources Committee on June 21, and S. 3524 was reported on July 12 by the Senate Finance Committee (S.Rept. 109-278). Concerns continue about some Medicaid and other federal reimbursements provisions, and other issues. Congress has also been asked to address the funding of contract support costs, used to pay administrative costs for tribes operating IHS-funded programs. Funding has usually been insufficient to cover all tribal contract support costs, which may lead tribes to use program funds to make up the difference, which in turn, some argue, means less health treatment offered at IHS-funded centers.

Chapter 2 - With the dramatic population increase in the West over the last thirty years, the Western states have been under increasing pressure from their citizens to secure future access to water. In planning to meet this goal, however, Western officials have had to confront a heretofore obscure doctrine of water law:

the doctrine of Indian reserved water rights, also known as the *Winters* doctrine. This doctrine holds that when Congress reserves land for an Indian reservation, Congress also reserves water to fulfill the purpose of the reservation. When this doctrine is applied to the water laws of the Western states, tribal rights to water are almost always senior to other claimants. Therefore, in order for Western water officials to effectively plan for a stable allocation of water on which all parties can rely, they must find a way to satisfy the water claims of local Indian tribes. The parties originally took to the courts to resolve these issues, only to find themselves in an endless cycle of litigation that rarely produced definitive rulings. As a result, negotiated settlements - which require Congressional authorization in order to be valid - are fast becoming the norm. This report provides an overview of the legal issues surrounding Indian reserved water rights disputes.

Chapter 3 - The Native American Graves Protection and Repatriation Act (NAGPRA) was enacted to serve as a means for museums and federal agencies to return certain Native American cultural items (including human remains) to the lineal descendants, culturally affiliated Indian tribes, or Native Hawaiian organizations. NAGPRA makes provision for both intentionally excavated and inadvertently discovered Native American cultural items on federal and tribal lands. Penalties are provided for noncompliance. A Review Committee was established by NAGPRA to monitor the various processes and to assist in dispute resolution involving repatriation issues.

Certain provisions of NAGPRA were judicially scrutinized in a series of cases concerning the disposition of the remains of an ancient man, believed to be about 9,000 years old and known as the Kennewick Man or the Ancient One, which was discovered on federal land under the jurisdiction of the U.S. Army Corps of Engineers ("COE"). The COE considered the applicability of NAGPRA to the situation, and concluded that NAGPRA was applicable. The COE proposed to return the remains to a coalition of Native American groups. This action was challenged by a group of scientists and others who successfully argued that the provisions of NAGPRA were not applicable. The U.S. Court of Appeals for the Ninth Circuit concluded in *Bonnichsen v. U.S.* that the remains were not identifiable with any current day Native American group, and therefore the provisions of NAGPRA did not apply.

An amendment to NAGPRA has been proposed in section 108 of S. 563, the "Native American Omnibus Act of 2005." If enacted, the amendment would define "Native American" within the context of NAGPRA so as to include a tribe, people, or culture that is or *was* indigenous to any geographic area that is now located within the boundaries of the United States. If enacted, the amendment could have an impact on the ultimate disposition of the remains of the Kennewick

Man, as well as the control and custody of any other ancient human remains and related objects which may be discovered.

Interest in NAGPRA is particularly strong during the summer of 2005, as severe weather conditions have caused various rivers in the continental United States–such as the Missouri River–to recede. This has exposed traditional Native American burial grounds which have been subject to increased looting and vandalism.

The Senate Committee on Indian Affairs held oversight hearings on NAGPRA for July 28, 2005. The hearings focused on the proposed amendment contained in S. 563.

Chapter 4 - On March 1, 2005, the Supreme Court handed down its decision in *Cherokee Nation of Oklahoma v. Leavitt*. The conflicts in the case (actually two consolidated cases) involved federal agencies' duty to fund contract support costs for contracts with Indian tribes under the Indian Self-Determination and Education Assistance Act (ISDA).

While the case in some ways turned on technical questions of statutory interpretation and appropriations law, it also presented interesting questions regarding the federal government's legal responsibility to honor ISDA contracts and how this responsibility compares to the government's general responsibility to pay contractors. This report includes background on the ISDA, a discussion of the conflicting appeals court decisions, and analysis of the Supreme Court's decision.

Chapter 5 - Native American issues before Congress are numerous and diverse, covering such areas as federal recognition of tribes, trust land acquisition, gambling regulation, education, jails, economic development, welfare reform, homeland security, tribal jurisdiction, highway construction, taxation, and many more. This report focuses on four Native American issues currently of great salience before Congress: health care, energy, trust fund management reform, and Native Hawaiian recognition.

Chapter 6 - In 1978, Congress enacted the Indian Child Welfare Act (ICWA) in response to legislative findings of harm caused to Indian children, their families, and tribes by the high separation rate of Indian children from their homes and cultural environments. Congress addressed this situation by granting Indian tribes and Indian parents an enhanced role in determining when to remove Indian children from their homes and cultural environments. Specifically, the ICWA enumerates provisions for tribal jurisdiction and tribal intervention in state court proceedings concerning the custody, adoption, foster care placement, and termination of parental rights of Indian children.

No bills amending the ICWA were introduced in the 109th Congress. Still, the debate over provisions of the ICWA remains an issue of concern. This CRS report provides an overview of some of the goals and provisions of the Indian Child Welfare Act.

Chapter 7 - The Indian Gaming Regulatory Act (IGRA) (P.L. 100-497) generally prohibits gaming on lands acquired for Indians in trust by the Secretary of the Interior (SOI) after the date of enactment of IGRA, October 17, 1988. The exceptions, however, may be significant because they raise the possibility of Indian gaming proposals for locations presently unconnected with an Indian tribe. Among the exceptions are land: (1) contiguous to or within reservation boundaries; (2) acquired after the SOI determines acquisition to be in the best interest of the tribe and not detrimental to the local community and the governor of the state concurs; (3) acquired for tribes that had no reservation on the date of enactment of IGRA; (4) acquired as part of a land claim settlement; (5) acquired as part of an initial reservation for a newly recognized tribe; and (6) acquired as part of the restoration of lands for a tribe restored to federal recognition. On October 5, 2006, the Bureau of Indian Affairs (BIA) of the Department of the Interior (DOI) issued a proposed regulation to specify the standards that must be satisfied by tribes seeking to conduct gaming on lands acquired after October 17, 1988. The proposal includes limiting definitions of some of the statutory terms and considerable specificity in the documentation required for such applications. Legislative proposals include H.R. 1654 and H.R. 2562, which contain provisions to tighten the standards for tribes to secure exceptions to IGRA's prohibition on gaming on lands acquired after 1988, and several bills dealing with recognition of particular tribes or transfers of specific pieces of property (S. 310/ H.R. 505, S. 375/H.R. 679, H.R. 28, H.R. 65, H.R. 106, H.R. 673, and H.R. 1294), which include provisions that preclude gaming.

Chapter 8 - On March 29, 2005, the Supreme Court issued its decision in *City of Sherrill v. Oneida Indian Nation of New York*, a case with serious implications for the State of New York's ability to regulate tribal lands within New York. A federal appeals court had ruled that the Oneida Indian Nation could, by purchasing former reservation lands illegally alienated from the tribe, reestablish the reservation status of those lands and thereby shield them from state taxation. The Supreme Court reversed this decision, holding that the passage of time between the illegal conveyance and the claim in this case barred the Oneidas' attempt to reassert sovereignty over the land in question.

Chapter 9 - The list of federally recognized Indian tribes is not a static one. The Department of the Interior's Bureau of Indian Affairs has an administrative process by which a group may establish itself as an Indian tribe and become eligible for the services and benefits accorded Indian tribes under federal law. The process requires extensive documentation, including verification of continuous existence as an Indian tribe since 1900, and generally takes considerable time. Final determinations are subject to judicial review.

Chapter 10 - Under the Federal Election Campaign Act (FECA), Indian tribes are subject to contribution limits applicable to "persons," as defined by the act. For the 2008 election cycle, these limits include $2,300 per election to a candidate, $28,500 per year to a political party's national committee, and $5,000 per year to a political action committee (PAC). The Federal Election Commission (FEC) has found, however, that FECA's $108,200 election cycle aggregate limit applicable to "individuals," as defined by the act, does not apply to Indian tribes (similar to FECA's treatment of other interest groups that operate through PACs and are also not subject to an aggregate limit). In addition, as most Indian tribes are unincorporated, they are not subject to the FECA ban on use of corporate treasury funds for contributions and expenditures in connection with federal elections. Hence, unlike corporations, most Indian tribes are not required to establish PACs in order to participate in federal elections. As the result of an FEC ruling, unlike PACs, Indian tribes are also not required to disclose the amounts and recipients of any contributions they make. With regard to unregulated soft money, Indian tribes may spend unlimited amounts of money on issue advocacy communications.

The Bipartisan Campaign Reform Act (BCRA) of 2002 made several significant changes to FECA, including increasing certain contribution limits from their previous levels. BCRA also prohibited any "person," which includes Indian tribes, from making soft money donations to political parties. While FECA prohibits corporations and unions from paying for broadcast issue advertisements that refer to federal candidates within 30 days of a primary or 60 days of a general election, labeled by BCRA as "electioneering communications," unincorporated Indian tribes are not subject to such a prohibition. However, if an Indian tribe sponsors an electioneering communication, regardless of its incorporation status, it is subject to disclosure requirements, including the identification of disbursements and donors over certain dollar amounts.

In: Native Americans: Rights, Laws... ISBN: 978-1-60456-202-6
Editor: C. P. Townsend, pp. 1-49 © 2008 Nova Science Publishers, Inc.

Chapter 1

INDIAN HEALTH SERVICE: HEALTH CARE DELIVERY, STATUS, FUNDING, AND LEGISLATIVE ISSUES[*]

Donna U. Vogt and Roger Walke

ABSTRACT

The Indian Health Service (IHS), an agency in the Department of Health and Human Services (HHS), funds health care for eligible American Indians/Alaskan Natives (AI/AN) through a system of programs and facilities located on or near Indian reservations and in certain urban areas. The IHS health delivery program is organized in 12 regional area offices and 167 local service units, and serves federal reservations, Indian communities, and urban Indians. In general, persons eligible for IHS services must be in IHS service areas and belong to federally recognized tribes.

The IHS-served population generally has a higher incidence of illness and premature mortality than the general U.S. population. Several annual IHS publications compare the health conditions and causes of death of the IHS service population with those for the general U.S. population. According to the latest of these, the average life expectancy at birth for the IHS service area population in 1996-1998 was 70.6 years, or 5.9 years less than the 76.5 years for the total U.S. 1997 population.

IHS appropriations are separated into two budget categories: health services and health facilities. For FY2006, the appropriations for health

---
[*] Excerpted from CRS Report RL33022, dated September 12, 2006.

services is $2.692 billion and for health facilities $353 million. Of the total appropriation of $3.045 billion, 88% is for health services and 12% for health facilities. Other sources of funding include reimbursements from Medicare, Medicaid, and private insurance. If Indians are eligible and are recipients of such programs, IHS becomes the residual payer or "the payer of last resort." This means that IHS pays only after all other sources of payment have been exhausted.

While a number of legislative issues concerning IHS face the 109th Congress, congressional committees have focused primarily on the reauthorization of the Indian Health Care Improvement Act (IHCIA), which provides specific statutory authority for many IHS programs. Thus far two bills (S. 1057 and H.R. 5312) have been introduced in the 109th Congress to reauthorize the IHCIA, and another bill (S. 3524) has been introduced to amend, or create, IHCIA provisions in the Social Security Act. Both reauthorization bills would increase tribal participation in negotiated rule-making, elevate the position of the Director of IHS within the HHS to the level of Assistant Secretary for Indian Health, expand health services, increase reimbursement options from other federal programs, and authorize other actions. S. 1057 was reported, amended, by the Senate Indian Affairs Committee on March 16 (S.Rept. 109-222), H.R. 5312 was ordered reported, amended, by the House Resources Committee on June 21, and S. 3524 was reported on July12 by the Senate Finance Committee (S.Rept. 109-278). Concerns continue about some Medicaid and other federal reimbursements provisions, and other issues. Congress has also been asked to address the funding of contract support costs, used to pay administrative costs for tribes operating IHS-funded programs. Funding has usually been insufficient to cover all tribal contract support costs, which may lead tribes to use program funds to make up the difference, which in turn, some argue, means less health treatment offered at IHS-funded centers.

INTRODUCTION

The Indian Health Service (IHS), part of the Public Health Service (PHS) of the Department of Health and Human Services (HHS), funds health services to about 1.8 million Indians, members of the nation's 561 federally recognized American Indian and Alaska Native (AI/AN) tribes in IHS service delivery areas.[1] Health services are available to eligible residents of reservations, of non-reservation areas of those counties that overlap or abut reservations, and of some urban areas with significant AI/AN population. Eligible Indians receive free IHS health services regardless of their ability to pay. The federal government considers its provision of these health services to be based on its trust responsibility for Indian tribes, a responsibility derived from federal treaties, statutes, court decisions, executive actions, and the Constitution (which assigns authority over Indian relations to Congress).[2] Congress, however, has only a moral obligation, not a legal one, to provide Indian health care.[3] The Supreme Court has rejected the idea (absent congressional statement to the contrary) that IHS is under an obligation to provide any specific health program to Indians.[4]

This report provides an overview of the Indian Health Service and how it provides for the health care problems and needs of AI/AN. It also shows IHS appropriations for recent years and discusses its current statutory authorities and legislative issues, including the reauthorization of the Indian Health Care Improvement Act (IHCIA) and several other policy issues.

HEALTH CARE DELIVERY

The delivery of health services and funding of tribal and urban Indian health programs by the federal government has developed over more than a century. (Appendix A provides a brief history of the Indian Health Service.)

Organization of the IHS Health Delivery System

Currently, the IHS health care delivery system, a largely rural system, is organized into 12 regional area offices and 167 local service units, and serves federal reservations, Indian communities in Oklahoma and California, and Indian, Eskimo (Inuit and Yupik), and Aleut communities in Alaska. Service units are made up of counties and parts of counties.[5] All counties in the national IHS service area are covered by one or more service units.[6] The map in figure 1 shows the counties served by IHS-funded programs, including both IHS service areas and IHS-funded urban projects. Looked at as a whole, the IHS national service area roughly matches the distribution of federal Indian reservations and communities, although in five states (Alaska, Arizona, Nevada, Oklahoma, and South Carolina) every county is served by IHS.

Range of Health Services
IHS health services include inpatient, ambulatory, dental, and preventive care. IHS not only provides general clinical health services, but also focuses on such special Indian health problems as maternal and child health, fetal alcohol syndrome, diabetes prevention and treatment, alcoholism and mental health, emergency medical services, hepatitis B, dental services, and others. IHS provides these services directly, and through tribes, tribal organizations, and urban Indian

organizations (often referred to as ITU).[7] In addition, both IHS and the tribes may contract for health services from private providers. IHS also funds some sanitation facilities for Indian communities.

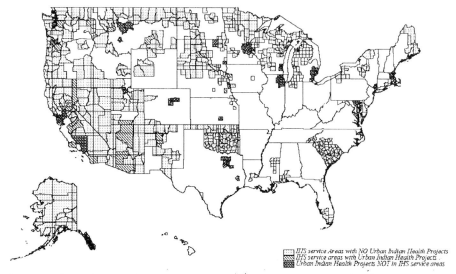

Source: Information provided by United States Geological Survey, National Atlas, and Indian Health Service. Map prepared by Library of Congress, Geography and Map Division, November 2001.

Figure 1. Counties Served by IHS-Funded Programs: IHS Service Areas and Urban Indian Health Projects.

Health Facilities

IHS-funded health care is provided in facilities managed both by IHS and by Indian tribes and tribal consortia. Through self-determination contracts and self-governance compacts negotiated with the IHS under the authority of the Indian Self-Determination and Education Assistance Act (P.L. 93-638; ISDEAA), tribes and tribal consortia have taken over from IHS the responsibility for operating service units and health facilities. (The ISDEAA is discussed at greater length below, under "Statutory Authority.") Currently, 504 of the 629 IHS-funded health facilities (80%) are operated by tribes under ISDEAA (see table 1).

Table 1. Number of Service Units and Facilities Operated by IHS and Tribes (As of October 1, 2004)

Type of facility	Total	IHS operated	Tribally operated		
			Total	Under ISDEAA contracts and compacts	Under non-ISDEAA contracts[a]
Hospitals	48	33	15	15	0
Ambulatory (out-patient) facilities	581	92	489	477	12
Health centers	272	52	220	216	4
School health centers	11	2	9	9	0
Health stations	136	38	98	97	1
Alaska village clinics	162	0	162	155	7
Health facilities, total	629	125	504	492	12
Service units	164	66	98	—	—

Source: U.S. Indian Health Service, personal communication, Feb. 27, 2006. Health facilities totals calculated by Congressional Research Service.

Notes: ISDEAA = Indian Self-Determination and Education Assistance Act (P.L. 93-638), as amended.

[a] Used in Alaska to fund Alaska Native-operated clinics not eligible for funding under ISDEAA. Sometimes these funding sources are called "non-638 contracts."

Contract Health Services

In addition to care received from IHS and tribal providers, health services are purchased by IHS and the tribes through contracts with more than 2,000 private providers, if the local facility is unable to provide the needed care.[8] Not all areas of the country are covered by this service. Areas where this IHS-funded contract health care is available are known as "contract health service delivery areas" (CHSDAs), and are the same as the IHS service areas shown in figure 1.

Urban Indian Health Projects

Although most IHS facilities are located on or near reservations, IHS also funds, with approximately 1% of its budget, 34 urban Indian health projects (UIHPs).[9] UIHPs are funded by IHS with grants and contracts and serve approximately 330,000 urban Indians living in IHS's urban service areas. Figure 1 also shows areas served by urban Indian health projects. Some urban projects are inside CHSDAs and some are not.

Other Health-Related Activities

IHS funds the construction, equipping, and maintenance of hospitals, health centers, clinics, and other health facilities, whether operated by IHS or tribes. Tribes may handle these activities under self-determination contracts or self-governance compacts.

Not only has IHS provided funding for health care delivery facilities, since 1960 it also has funded the construction of water supply and sewage facilities, solid waste disposal systems, and technical assistance for the operation and maintenance of such facilities, under the authority of the Indian Sanitation Facilities Act.[10] Currently, according to IHS, about 12% of AI/AN homes lack safe drinking water supplies and adequate waste disposal facilities, compared to about 1% of all U.S. homes.[11] Because of access to new sanitation facilities, there has been a 80% reduction in gastrointestinal disease among AI/AN since 1973.[12]

Limitations in Health Services

IHS does not provide the same health care services in each area. Services vary from place to place and from time to time.[13] In general, the services provided to any particular Indian community will depend on financial resources (i.e., appropriations and third party reimbursements) and available personnel and facilities.[14] IHS states that its funding does not allow it to provide all the needed care for eligible Indians.[15] As a result, according to Indian health organizations, some services are "rationed," with the most critical care given first.[16] IHS regulations require that, when resources or funds are insufficient, the agency must set priorities for both direct and contract health care based on "relative medical need."[17] In addition, the drugs and medicines available from IHS pharmacies may not include all drugs and medicines needed, although IHS says its pharmacies will stock most drugs that have proven to be cost-effective and beneficial.[18]

IHS shortfalls in medical personnel contribute to this unevenness in health care delivery. According to IHS data, in March 2005 it had job vacancy rates of 24% for dentists, 20% for medical imaging personnel, 14% for nurses, and 11% for physicians and pharmacists.[19]

Eligible Population

In general, persons eligible for IHS services are members of federally recognized tribes. They must also live on or near federal Indian reservations or in traditional Indian communities, or within a county where IHS contract health services are available. Eligible Indians include those of Indian descent belonging to the Indian community who are regarded as Indian by the community in which they live. Eligibility also is indicated by: (1) location within an IHS health service delivery area; (2) residence on tax-exempt land or ownership of property on land for which the federal government has a trust responsibility; (3) active participation in tribal affairs; or (4) meeting other relevant factors in keeping with general Bureau of Indian Affairs (BIA) practices in the jurisdiction for determining eligibility.[20] Urban Indian health programs funded by IHS may serve a wider range of eligible persons, including members of terminated[21] or state-recognized tribes and their children and grandchildren.[22]

In addition, eligible persons may also include a non-Indian woman pregnant with an eligible Indian's child. She would be eligible for care during the pregnancy and six weeks following birth, as long as paternity is acknowledged. The IHS also serves non-Indians in specific circumstances particularly when an acute infectious disease is involved.[23]

Most IHS services are intended for members of federally-recognized tribes. Since federal law does not restrict state recognition of tribes, some states grant recognition to Indian groups that are not recognized by the federal government. Members of such state-recognized tribes are ineligible for most IHS health services, but are eligible for services at IHS-funded urban Indian health projects.

For the most part, tribal membership is determined by the tribe. Many tribes require recognized descent from a particular tribal roll for membership. In tracing descent, tribes follow paternal or maternal bloodlines, or both. Some tribes require minimum percentages of genealogical descent, and others require only proof of descent. For a few tribes, Congress has set membership criteria in statute.[24]

The IHS service population is not evenly distributed throughout Indian country. Approximately 35% of the population served by IHS resides in two IHS administrative regional areas: the Navajo region (northeastern Arizona, northwestern New Mexico, and southeastern Utah, less the Hopi Reservation), with 14.4%, and the Oklahoma region (Kansas, Oklahoma, and part of Texas), with 20.7%.[25]

Population Data

Determining the actual number of people eligible for IHS services is problematic. There is no U.S. census of members of federally-recognized tribes (or, for that matter, of members of terminated and state-recognized tribes who might be eligible for UIHP services). IHS makes annual estimates of its eligible "service population" based on decennial census data, adjusted for birth and death rates and for the areas IHS serves (see figure 1).[26] The census, however, asks respondents only to identify themselves by race,[27] not by confirmed membership in a federally-recognized tribe.[28] Hence IHS service population data are based on self-identification as AI/AN by race, not on tribal membership. Not all persons self-identifying as AI/AN are members of federally-recognized tribes, so not all AI/AN counted by the census are eligible for IHS services. The IHS also estimates its "user population," based on registered AI/AN patients who used IHS-funded services at least once in the most recent three years,[29] but this figure does not include all eligible AI/AN. The BIA publishes biennial estimates of its own service population, based on estimates received from federally-recognized tribes, but the estimates are not based on actual censuses and cover only persons on or near reservations.[30] BIA has recently added tribes' reports of their total enrollment, but BIA conducts no census to confirm these figures, and its publication does not show whether the enrollees enumerated live on or near reservations or inside or outside IHS service areas. Table 2 below compares recent IHS, BIA, and census population figures.

Determining the *urban* Indian population eligible for UIHP services is equally problematic. As noted above, UIHPs serve a wider range of eligible persons, including members of terminated or state-recognized tribes and their children and grandchildren. They are not, however, authorized to serve anyone who merely identifies themselves as racially Indian.[31] BIA figures for service population and tribal enrollment, in addition to the problems already mentioned, are not broken down by urban or metropolitan residence. While census data for AI/AN are broken down by urban, metropolitan, city, and other types of residence, they are still, as noted above, based on self-identification by race, not on tribal membership, whether in federal, state, or terminated tribes. IHS figures for urban Indian populations are based on these Census data.

While IHS, Census, and BIA figures for Indians, whether resident in urban areas or not, may not be definitive for the IHS-eligible population, they undoubtedly provide useful approximations of the population that IHS serves. Census data suggest that most AI/AN live outside reservations and other census-identified Indian areas, that the movement out of these areas is many decades old, and that a majority of census-identified Indians live in census-identified urban areas.[32] Many urban areas are within CHSDAs, however, so further analysis may be needed to determine what proportion of census-identified urban Indians are eligible for general IHS services.

HEALTH STATUS

Comparisons of health and morbidity measures show that the IHS-served population generally has a higher incidence of illness and premature mortality than the general U.S. population. The differences in mortality rates have diminished in recent years in such areas as infant and maternal mortality, and mortality associated with alcoholism, injuries, tuberculosis, gastroenteritis, and other conditions. In contrast with statistics for the general U.S. population, Indians have a 738% greater chance of dying from alcoholism, a 500% greater chance of dying from tuberculosis, a 391% greater chance of dying from diabetes, and a 315% greater chance of dying from accidents. (See table 3.) One reason, according to the IHS, for the poor health status of many AI/AN is that many Indians have less access to health care than do people in the general U.S. population. Several annual IHS publications compare the health conditions and causes of death of the IHS service population with those for the general U.S. population. In addition, one of them compares IHS 1996-1998 average data with U.S. 1997 population data. The average life expectancy at birth for the IHS service area population in 1996-1998 was 70.6 years, or 5.9 years less than the 76.5 years for the total U.S. 1997 population.[33] The higher mortality rate for a number of leading causes of death among AI/AN is related to alcohol abuse, including not only alcohol-related deaths but also accidents, suicide, and homicide.

Diabetes[34]
AI/AN suffer from a disproportionately high and growing rate of Type 2 diabetes with its prevalence increasing 41% between 1997 and 2003 in all service areas, and particularly among young adults aged 25-34 years. In fact, between 1990 and 2003 the incidence of diabetes among these young AI/AN adults grew 135%.[35] Diabetes mortality is 3.1 times higher in the AI/AN than in the general U.S. population.[36] Diabetes is also a major cause of AI/AN morbidity, leading to blindness, kidney failure, lower-extremity amputation, and cardiovascular disease.[37]

Table 2. Differing Indian Population Figures, Selected Years, 1990-2004

Year	Indian Health Service		Bureau of Indian Affairs		Census Bureau	
	Service population (in IHS service areas) (est.)	User population (at IHS facilities)	Service population (on or near reservations) (est.)	Tribal enrollment (national) (est.)	AI/AN race alone	AI/AN race alone or in combination with other races
1990	1,207,236	1,104,693	—	—	Decennial: 1,959,234 race alone	—
1991	1,242,745	1,134,655	1,001,606	—	—	—
1997	1,427,453	1,300,634	1,442,747	1,654,433	—	—
1999	1,489,341	—	1,397,931	1,698,483	—	—
2000	1,515,594	—	—	—	Decennial: 2,475,956	4,119,301
2001	1,542,450	1,345,242	1,524,025	1,816,504	Estimates: 2,673,462	4,236,378
2003	Projections: 1,594,433	1,383,664	1,587,519	1,923,650	Estimates: 2,711,452	4,279,971
2004	1,771,431	1,415,197	—	—	Estimates: 2,786,691	4,366,011
					Estimates: 2,824,751	4,409,446

Sources: IHS service population, 1990-2003: IHS, *Trends in Indian Health*, 1998-2003, various pages. IHS service population, 2004: IHS, personal communication, Feb. 22, 2006. IHS user population, 1990-2001: IHS, *Regional Differences in Indian Health*, 1992-2001, various pages. IHS user population, 2003: IHS, *IHS Budget Breakout — Medical and Non-Medical [for 2003]*. IHS user population, 2004: IHS, personal communication, Feb. 22, 2006. All IHS publications are authored by U.S. Department of Health and Human Services, Public Health Service, Indian Health Service, Office of Planning, Evaluation, and Legislation, Division of Program Statistics, and published in Rockville, MD. BIA service population, 1991: *Indian Service Population and Labor Force Estimates* (1991), table 1 (recalculated by CRS). BIA service population and tribal enrollment, 1997: *Indian Labor Force Report: Portrait 1997*, "National Totals" table. BIA service population and tribal enrollment, 1999: *Indian Labor Force Report, 1999*, "National Totals" table. BIA service population and tribal enrollment, 2001: *Indian Labor Force Report, 2001*, "National Totals" table. BIA service population and tribal enrollment, 2003: *Indian Labor Force Report, 2003*, "National Totals" table. All BIA publications are authored by U.S. Department of the Interior, Bureau of Indian Affairs, and published in Washington, D.C. Census Bureau: 1990-2000 (April 1): U.S. Bureau of the Census, American Factfinder website [http://factfinder.census.gov/home/saff/main.html?_lang=en]; 2001-2004 (July 1): Population Estimates [http://www.census.gov/popest/national/asrh/ NC-EST2004-srh.html].

Table 3. Mortality Rates for IHS Service Population and U.S. Population (All Races), Total and for Selected Causes, 1996-1998 (Age-adjusted rates per 100,000 population)

Cause of death	IHS service population (average 1996-1998)	U.S. all races (1997)	IHS rate as percentage of U.S. rate
All causes	715.2	479.1	149%
Alcohol-related	46.5	6.3	738%
Tuberculosis	1.5	0.3	500%
Diabetes	52.8	13.5	391%
Accidents (unintentional injury, including motor vehicle)	94.7	30.1	315%
Injury and poisoning	2.7	1.3	208%
Suicide	20.2	10.6	191%
Homicide	14.5	8.0	181%
Pneumonia and influenza	21.5	12.9	167%
Firearm injury	17.6	12.2	144%
Gastrointestinal diseases	1.8	1.3	138%
Heart diseases	157.1	130.5	120%
Cerebrovascular diseases (affecting blood supply to the brain)	29.5	25.9	114%
Cancers (malignant neoplasms)	124.0	125.6	99%
Cervical cancer (females)	4.2	2.5	168%
Lung cancer	37.4	33.5	112%
Prostate cancer (males)	11.5	13.9	83%
Breast cancer (females)	15.6	19.4	80%
HIV (human immunodeficiency virus) infection	3.3	5.8	57%
Birth-related mortality			
Maternal mortality (per 100,000 live births)	6.8	8.4	81%
Infant mortality (per 1,000 live births)	8.9	7.2	124%

Source: IHS, *Trends in Indian Health 2000-2001*, parts 3 and 4, various tables.
Note: The AI/AN mortality rates are age-adjusted to the national 1940 standard population, and are then computed by applying the age-specific death rate for a given cause of death using the AI/AN population residing in counties that make up the IHS service area. The rates were also adjusted for the miscoding of Indian race on death certificates.

With the 1997 Balanced Budget Act, Congress began a Special Diabetes Program for Indians (SDPI) as part of IHS's ongoing National Diabetes Program. With SDPI grant monies, tribal health programs, urban Indian health programs, and IHS have set up diabetes programs to create an extensive support network that gives training, "best practices," and the latest scientific findings with area diabetes consultants, model diabetes programs and other grant programs in 318 AI/AN communities in 35 states.[38] The funding has enhanced patient care and education and created a needed infrastructure for diabetes programs. With the funding, IHS, Urban Indian Organizations (UIOs), and tribes are able to support prevention programs which have been shown to delay the onset of the disease through lifestyle changes or use of the medication.[39] The program's disease performance measures have tracked the success of the SDPI efforts to fight diabetes. So far the program's efforts have seen an increase of diabetics maintaining blood sugar control from 25% in FY1997 to 34% in FY2004. In addition, there are other decreases in the number of health incidents related to diabetes including kidney disease and retinopathy. Other programs are tying diabetes screening with other diseases. For example, on May 16, 2005, the National Institutes of Health announced the beginning of an educational campaign to promote the message that AI/AN can reduce the risk of a heart attack or stroke if they keep under control their blood glucose, blood pressure, and cholesterol.[40]

APPROPRIATIONS AND FUNDING

IHS funding is separated into four budget categories: health services, facilities, collections (reimbursements from Medicare and Medicaid, as well as private insurance), and SDPI. Health services and facilities appropriations constitute IHS's budget authority; its budget authority plus collections and SDPI constitute IHS's program-level funding. Table 4 below shows detailed funding for IHS programs for FY2000-FY2006, with the request for FY2007.[41] Figure 2 shows the trends in IHS budget authority and program-level funding for FY1995-FY2006, in current dollars and constant 1994 dollars.[42]

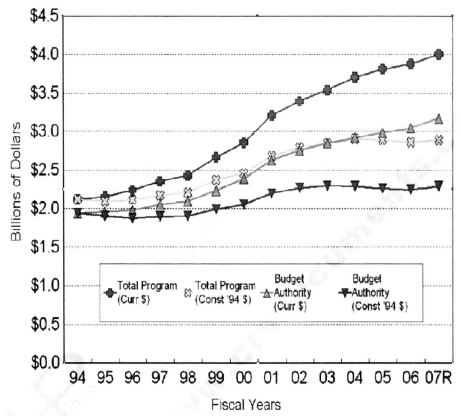

Sources: Prepared by the Congressional Research Service from appropriations and collections data provided by IHS, with Consumer Price Index[42] data provided in U.S. President, *The Economic Report of the President, 2006* (Feb. 2006) and U.S. Congressional Budget Office, *The Budget and Economic Outlook: Fiscal Years 2007 to 2016* (Jan. 2006).
Note: R = Request.

Figure 2. IHS Funding: Total Program Funding and Budget Authority, in Current and Constant 1994 Dollars, FY1994-FY2007R.

Collections

Indians are U.S. citizens and hence many are eligible for Medicare and Medicaid.[43] Congress has authorized IHS and tribes operating IHS-funded health facilities to collect reimbursements from Medicare and Medicaid (see "Statutory Authority," below). Collections funding has grown from 9% of the IHS program-level budget in FY1995 to 18% in FY2006. Since many Indians on or near reservations lack employment-related health insurance benefits, IHS collections come mostly from the Medicaid and Medicare programs, of which Medicaid provides the majority. Medicaid grew from 55% of collections in FY1995 to 70% from FY2002 on. "Overall," says IHS, "Medicaid and Medicare collections represent up to 50% of the hospital and clinic operating budgets."[44]

Diabetes Funding

In the Balanced Budget Act of 1997 (P.L. 105-33), Congress created two programs for diabetes: the IHS's SDPI and the National Institutes of Health (NIH) Special Research Program for Type 1 Diabetes. The law required that the State Children's Health Insurance Program (SCHIP) appropriation for FY1998 through FY2002 be reduced by $60 million each year, with $30 million allocated to SDPI and $30 million going to the NIH Type 1 Diabetes research program. In 2000, the Benefits Improvement and Protection Act (part of P.L. 106-534) increased funding for each of these diabetes programs and extended authority for grants to be made under both. For each grant program, total funding was increased to $100 million for FY2001, FY2002, and FY2003. For FY2001 and FY2002, $30 million of the $100 million for each program came from the SCHIP program appropriation and $70 million came from the general Treasury. In FY2003 the whole $100 million for each program was drawn from the general Treasury.

In December 2002, Congress in P.L. 107-360 extended the funding for these special diabetes programs and authorized $150 million for each of the programs each year for FY2004-FY2008. This funding from the general Treasury is separate from regular IHS and NIH appropriations (as noted in table 4).

Funding Disparities

Groups supporting Indian health care have argued that IHS per capita expenditures on health services are often less than per capita expenditures in other federal health-related programs. The private nonprofit National Indian Health Board, for example, pointed out that, in FY1997, IHS's per capita expenditures were $1,430 as compared with $3,489 per capita under the federal Bureau of Prisons (BOP) and $5,458 under the Department of Veterans Affairs (VA).[45] Three years later, however, in FY2000, IHS per capita spending had risen 11% to $1,582,[46] while BOP's had fallen 19% to $2,840[47] and VA's had fallen 7% to $5,063.[48] Comparisons of per capita spending under different federal health programs are problematic, however, because — as with BOP and VA — the programs may serve different populations, with differing demographic characteristics and health needs, and may provide different sets of health care services.

Table 4. Indian Health Service Funding, FY2000-2007R
(in millions of dollars)

	FY2000	FY2001	FY2002	FY2003	FY2004	FY2005	FY2006	FY2007R
Budget Authority (total)	$2,390.7	$2,628.8	$2,758.1	$2,849.7	$2,921.7	$2,985.1	$3,045.3	$3,169.8
Health Services (subtotal):	$2,074.2	$2,265.7	$2,388.6	$2,475.9	$2,530.4	$2,596.5	$2,692.1	$2,822.5
Clinical Services:	$1,632.3	$1,796.2	$1,891.4	$1,973.8	$2,024.9	$2,090.6	$2,176.2	$2,323.3
Hospitals and Health Clinics	$1,005.4	$1,084.2	$1,153.2	$1,212.0	$1,249.8	$1,289.4	$1,339.5	$1,429.8
Dental Health	$80.1	$91.0	$95.3	$99.6	$104.5	$109.0	$117.7	$127.0
Mental Health	$43.2	$45.0	$47.1	$50.3	$53.3	$55.1	$58.5	$61.7
Alcohol and Substance Abuse	$96.8	$130.3	$135.0	$136.8	$138.3	$139.1	$143.2	$150.6
Contract Health Services	$406.8	$445.8	$460.8	$475.0	$479.1	$498.1	$517.3	$554.3
Preventive Health:	$91.9	$95.7	$99.7	$102.6	$106.9	$110.4	$117.1	$125.0
Public Health Nursing	$34.5	$36.1	$37.8	$39.6	$42.6	$45.0	$49.0	$53.0
Health Education	$9.6	$10.1	$10.6	$11.0	$11.8	$12.4	$13.6	$14.5
Community Health Reps	$46.4	$48.1	$49.8	$50.4	$51.0	$51.4	$52.9	$55.8
Immunization (Alaska)	$1.4	$1.5	$1.5	$1.5	$1.6	$1.6	$1.6	$1.7
Urban Indian Health	$27.8	$29.8	$30.9	$31.3	$31.6	$31.8	$32.7	$0
Indian Health Professions	$30.5	$30.5	$31.2	$31.1	$30.8	$30.4	$31.0	$31.7
Tribal Management	$2.4	$2.4	$2.4	$2.4	$2.4	$2.3	$2.4	$2.5
Direct Operations	$51.0	$52.9	$54.8	$60.2	$60.7	$61.6	$62.2	$63.8
Self Governance	FY2000	$9.8	$9.9	$5.6	$5.6	$5.6	$5.7	$5.8
Contract Support Costs	$9.5	$248.2	$268.2	$269.0	$267.4	$263.7	$264.7	$270.3
Facilities (subtotal):	$228.8	$363.1	$369.5	$373.7	$391.4	$388.6	$353.2	$347.3
Maintenance and Improvement	$316.6	$46.3	$46.3	$49.5	$48.9	$49.2	$51.6	$52.7
Sanitation Facilities	$43.4	$93.6	$93.8	$93.2	$93.0	$91.8	$92.1	$94.0
Health Care Facilities Construction	$92.1	$85.5	$86.3	$81.6	$94.6	$88.6	$37.8	$17.7
Facilities & Environmental Health Support	$50.4	$121.3	$126.8	$132.3	$137.8	$141.7	$150.7	$161.3
Equipment	$116.3	$16.3	$16.3	$17.2	$17.1	$17.3	$20.9	$21.6
Collections (total)	$14.3	$479.5	$534.8	$591.7	$634.4	$677.6	$684.1	$684.1

Table 4. (Continued).

	FY2000	FY2001	FY2002	FY2003	FY2004	FY2005	FY2006	FY2007R
Medicare	$437.0	$114.7	$109.4	$119.2	$129.4	$136.5	$137.0	$137.0
Medicaid	$109.1	$316.1	$375.3	$417.7	$446.0	$472.5	$478.5	$478.5
Private Insurance	$283.3	$43.1	$44.4	$48.9	$52.8	$62.4	$62.4	$62.4
Program level (grand total)	$30.0	$3,208.2	$3,392.9	$3,541.4	$3,706.1	$3,812.6	$3,879.4	$4,003.9

Source: Data files from June Tracy, Legislative and Congressional Affairs, Office of the Director, Indian Health Service, U.S. Department of Health and Human Services, Mar. 24 and May 10, 2005; CRS Report RL32893, *Interior, Environment, and Related Agencies: FY2006 Appropriations*; and U.S. Department of Health and Human Services, Indian Health Service, *Justification of Estimates for Appropriations Committees, Fiscal Year 2007*, Feb. 2006, p. 13.

Notes: Appropriations are after supplemental appropriations and rescissions. R = Request.

A multi-part study initiated in 1998 showed the disparities that exist in personal medical services between IHS and mainstream health care systems.[49] Initially called the "Level of Need Funded" (LNF) study, and retitled the "FEHBP Disparity Index" (FDI) study, the study was produced by a workgroup of 16 people (15 tribal representatives and one IHS official) charged with the responsibility by IHS, and assisted by experts and consultants. The workgroup chose the Federal Employees Health Benefits Plan (FEHBP) as the benchmark mainstream personal medical services plan against which to compare IHS health services.[50]

The FDI study found that in FY2000, the total cost to give each AI/AN in the IHS user population coverage comparable with that received by federal employees under the FEHBP would be $3,221 per AI/AN. Of this amount, $2,431 would be from IHS appropriations and the rest from reimbursement programs such as Medicare, Medicaid, and private insurance. FEHBP-level coverage for the 1.43 million IHS user population, according to the FDI study, would call for IHS appropriations of about $3.5 billion in FY2000 for personal medical services.

The study found that actual FY2000 IHS appropriations for personal medical services would provide just over 50% of the appropriations needed to give IHS users personal medical services equivalent to the FEHBP, and that an additional $1.7 billion would be needed to raise the level of IHS's coverage to 100% of the FEHBP's.

The study also found funding variations within the Indian health system — estimating, for instance, that 112 of the 244 operating units identified in the study are funded below the IHS-wide average of 50% of FEHBP services.[51] The FDI results for 2000 also suggested that the urban Indian health program funded 4% of needed resources in FY2000, according to the IHS.[52]

The IHS has previously identified funding shortfalls in other service areas. For instance, facilities maintenance was funded at 27.5% of need for FY2004; replacement of biomedical equipment was funded at about 20% of need in FY2004; sanitation facilities for new homes is funded at 70%, and for existing homes at 5%, of need in FY2005; and health professions scholarships are projected to be funded at 10% of new applications in FY2005.[53]

STATUTORY AUTHORITY AND COMMITTEE JURISDICTION

Over the last eight decades, Congress has enacted a number of statutes providing general or specific authorizations for health services to AI/ANs. Before that, Congress directed the BIA to provide Indian health care and construct Indian health facilities, through annual Indian appropriations acts.

Statutory Authority

Currently, the IHS administers funds and policies under several statutes.

Snyder Act of 1921[54]
This act provides a broad and permanent authorization for federal Indian programs, including for "conservation of health." All such programs were at the time under the management of the BIA. The act was passed because Congress had never enacted any specific statutory authorizations for most of the many BIA activities that had developed since the Civil War as more and more tribes were placed on reservations. Instead, Congress had made detailed annual appropriations for BIA activities. Authority for Indian appropriations in the House had been assigned to the Indian Affairs Committee after 1885 (and in the Senate to its Indian Affairs Committee after 1899). Rules changes in the House in 1920, however, moved Indian appropriations authority to the Appropriations Committee, making Indian appropriations vulnerable to procedural objections because they lacked authorizing acts. The Snyder Act was passed in order to authorize all the activities the BIA was then carrying out. The act's broad language, however, may be read as authorizing — though not requiring — nearly any Indian program, including health care, for which Congress enacts appropriations.

Transfer Act of 1954[55]
The act transferred the responsibility for Indian health care from the BIA to the Public Health Service (PHS) in the newly-established Department of Health, Education and Welfare (now HHS). Among other reasons, Congress felt the PHS could do a better job of providing health care services to Indians.

Indian Sanitation Facilities Act of 1959[56]
This act, amending the Transfer Act, authorizes the PHS to construct sanitation facilities for Indian communities and homes.

Indian Self-Determination and Education Assistance Act (ISDEAA) of 1975[57]

ISDEAA, as amended, provides for tribal administration of federal Indian programs, especially BIA and IHS programs. The act allows tribes to assume some control over the management of their health care services by negotiating "self-determination contracts" with IHS for tribal management of specific IHS programs. Under a self-determination contract, IHS transfers to tribal control the funds it would have spent for the contracted program so the tribe might operate the program. Under ISDEAA authority, IHS has also established a tribal consultation policy giving tribes an opportunity to help formulate health priorities in the President's annual budget request.

Tribal Self-Governance Program

Beginning in 1992, Congress amended ISDEAA to allow tribal governments to consolidate IHS self-determination contracts for multiple IHS programs into a single "self-governance compact." Under a self-governance compact, the same transfer of IHS funds and operating control takes place as happens with a self-determination contract, but the compacting tribe is authorized to redesign programs and services and to reallocate funds for those programs and services. BIA programs had been authorized for compacting under a demonstration program in 1988,[58] and similar authority was extended to IHS programs in 1992.[59] In 2000, the Tribal Self-Governance Amendments[60] made the IHS self-governance program permanent, as Title V of ISDEAA.

Indian Health Care Improvement Act (IHCIA) of 1976[61]

IHCIA authorizes many specific IHS activities, sets out the national policy for health services administered to AI/AN, and sets health condition goals for the IHS service population in order to raise the health status of AI/AN to the highest possible level. Most significantly, IHCIA authorizes direct collections from Medicare/Medicaid and third party insurers. It also gives IHS authority to grant funding to urban Indian organizations to provide health care services to urban Indians and established substance abuse treatment programs, Indian health professions recruitment programs, and many other programs.

Alaska Native and American Indian Direct Reimbursement Act of 2000[62]

This act amended IHCIA to make permanent a demonstration program for direct billing of Medicare and Medicaid by AI/AN health organizations with self-determination contracts or self-governance compacts. The demonstration program, involving four tribally operated IHS-owned hospitals and clinics, had increased collections, reduced the turn-around time between billing and receipt of payment, eased tracking of billings and collections, and reduced administrative costs.

Congressional Committee Jurisdiction

Currently a number of committees hold jurisdiction over legislation affecting the Indian Health Service. In general, legislation amending an existing statute is likely to be referred to the committees that held jurisdiction over the original legislation.

House Jurisdiction
Major jurisdiction over Native American issues, Indian health care legislation, and self-governance is held by the Resources Committee. In matters of public health care and health facilities legislation and programs such as Medicaid, Medicare Part B, and SCHIP, the Energy and Commerce Committee has jurisdiction. However, Energy and Commerce shares jurisdiction with the Committee on Ways and Means for legislation dealing with Medicare, Part B. The Committee on Ways and Means has exclusive jurisdiction over Medicare Part A. Bills to reauthorize IHCIA have been referred to the Committee on Resources, and, in addition, to the Committees on Energy and Commerce and Ways and Means for consideration of provisions that come under their jurisdiction. Recent IHCIA reauthorization bills also contain a provision to elevate the IHS director to the level of an assistant secretary within HHS; reauthorization bills with this provision were referred to the Committee on Government Reform in the 107th Congress, but not in the 108th or 109th Congresses.

Senate Jurisdiction
In general, the Committee on Indian Affairs holds jurisdiction over all Senate legislation relating to Indians. The Senate Health, Education, Labor and Pensions Committee has jurisdiction over matters of public health and the Senate Finance Committee has jurisdiction over Medicare, Medicaid and SCHIP. Recent Senate IHCIA reauthorization bills have been referred to the Indian Affairs Committee alone, but in the 109th Congress a bill relating to provisions in the Social Security Act added by IHCIA, regarding Medicaid and Medicare, was referred only to the Finance Committee.

Appropriations Jurisdiction

Although IHS is part of the Public Health Service of HHS, its annual appropriation is under the jurisdiction of the Interior and environment subcommittees of the Appropriation Committees, in both houses.

CURRENT LEGISLATIVE ISSUES

There are a number of Indian health issues that have been or likely will be debated in the 109th Congress. Foremost is the reauthorization of the IHCIA (and related amendments to the Social Security Act (SSA)).

Reauthorization of the Indian Health Care Improvement Act

Although many IHS programs are permanently authorized by the general language of the Snyder Act, the IHCIA added a number of more detailed authorizations for other programs and inserted Indian provisions in the SSA. IHCIA's specific authorizations of appropriations expired at the end of FY2001, although Congress continues to appropriate funds for its programs.

The current Senate IHCIA reauthorization bill, S. 1057, was introduced on May 17, 2005, and reported, with amendments, by the Senate Indian Affairs Committee on March 16, 2006 (S.Rept. 109-222).[63] Another Senate bill, S. 3524, which addressed only IHCIA amendments to the SSA, was introduced June 15, 2006, and reported July 12 by the Senate Finance Committee with the intention that S. 3524's provisions be incorporated into S. 1057 when the latter bill is considered on the Senate floor.[64] A House IHCIA reauthorization bill very similar to S. 1057 as reported, H.R. 5312, was introduced May 9, 2006, and referred to the Resources Committee, as well as to the Energy and Commerce Committee and the Ways and Means Committee for provisions within their jurisdictions. The Resources Committee ordered H.R. 5312 reported, with amendments, on June 21, 2006, but a printed report has not been published as of this writing.

IHCIA reauthorization has been under consideration since 1999. Reauthorization bills were introduced in the 106th (H.R. 3397 and S. 2526), 107th (S. 212 and H.R. 1662), and 108th (S. 556 and H.R. 2440) Congresses. Negotiations among Indian health proponents, HHS agencies, the Administration, and congressional committees and offices have led to numerous changes in the bills from one Congress to the next. Extensive hearings have been held on all bills, but only in the 108th and 109th Congresses have bills been reported from committee.

S. 1057, as reported, and H.R. 5312, as introduced, would make numerous significant changes to current law. They would elevate the head of IHS to an assistant secretary position; expand the roles of tribes, tribal organizations (TOs), and urban Indian organizations (UIOs) in management and decision-making; organize behavioral health services (alcohol and substance abuse, social services, and mental health programs) into a "comprehensive continuum" of prevention and treatment programs; create a construction priority system for IHS-funded health facilities; authorize long-term and hospice care; exempt Indians from Medicaid and SCHIP premiums and copayments; allow urban Indian health programs (UIHPs) to get reimbursements from Medicare and other third parties; establish a commission on how to improve Indian health care delivery; and add negotiated-rulemaking requirements to many programs. While retaining the same general structure of current law, the bills would rearrange many existing sections so that provisions dealing with similar topics, such as mental health or third-party reimbursements, are in the same title. The bills would also centralize separate appropriations authorizations, now scattered within each of the act's titles, into one general authorization of appropriations for each title, and authorize appropriations through FY2015.

Issues and provisions are discussed below in their general order of occurrence in the bills.

Definitions

The bills add or amend many of the definitions used in the act. Some of the changes may have program or policy implications, discussed below.

Expansion of Services

The bills greatly expand the definitions of "health promotion" and "disease prevention," which increases the range of services that Indians may demand of IHS, since the terms occur frequently in IHCIA. For instance, the bills would require that the HHS Secretary "shall provide health promotion and disease prevention services to Indians" (§203(b)). "Health promotion" would be expanded from seven items to 34 and would include such general activities as "improving the physical, economic, cultural, psychological, and social environment" and "promoting adequate opportunity for spiritual, religious, and traditional health care practices," as well as a lengthy list of more specific programs, such as abuse prevention, community health, and safe work environments (§4(11)). The definition of "disease prevention" would be expanded to include limitation and prevention of disease in general, not just of specific conditions (§4(9)). IHS and HHS may not have the funding or ability to provide all such expanded services (e.g., "safe housing" or a "safe work environment").[65]

Recipients

The bills would add several new terms for Indian health services managed by various entities: "Tribal Health Program" and "Indian Health Program." The term Tribal Health Program (THP) is defined as a tribe or TO that operates a health program or facility funded partly or wholly by the IHS under an ISDEAA funding agreement (§4(25)). An Indian Health Program (IHP) is defined as any Indian health program administered directly by the IHS, by a THP, or by a tribe or TO with HHS funding under the Buy Indian Act[66] (§4(13)). Many references to tribes and TOs in current law are changed to THPs in the bills; similarly, references to the IHS, tribes, and TOs in current law are changed to IHPs. Current law already authorizes TOs or tribes to operate some IHS-funded programs, but in the bills the new terms often expand the types of entities eligible to receive funding or administer programs.

Traditional Health Care

S. 1057 in several sections authorizes or directs IHS to fund traditional Indian health care practices and practitioners. It defines "traditional health care practices" as "the application by Native healing practitioners of the Native healing sciences" as opposed to western medicine (§4(23)). H.R. 5312 contains no definition of traditional health care practices, but includes many program references to traditional practices.

Indian Health Professional and Human Resources

As in current law, Title I of both bills covers personnel recruitment, scholarships, and other educational programs. The purpose of this title is to increase the number, and enhance the skills, of Indian and non-Indian health professionals and other health personnel in the IHS. To do this, the act authorizes scholarships for preparatory and professional schools. The bills add UIO programs and employees, where possible, to be eligible for involvement with training. They also expand the right to a "retention bonus" to all health professionals employed in or assigned to IHP or UIO programs. They eliminate nursing school clinics and restrict the existing community-college health training programs to accredited community colleges on or near reservations.

Community Health

Title I of the bills also reauthorizes two programs, the Community Health Representative Program and the Community Health Aide/Practitioner (CHAP) program in Alaska. These two programs not only recruit and train health representatives and aides, but also authorize them to provide health care, health promotion, and disease prevention services (including some dental services) to Indian communities, especially rural communities that have difficulty accessing health services. A new provision in the CHAP authorization in the bills authorizes a national CHAP program, although excluding certain community dental health services.

Community Dental Health Services

The Alaska CHAP program recently started a new Alaska Dental Health Aide Program.[67] The program seeks to provide access to dental care for residents of remote Alaskan villages which cannot support full-time dentists. It expands an existing CHAP program, which trains aides in dental education, dental assistance, and preventive dental services, to allow the aides to be trained as dental health aide *therapists*, who can perform more complicated dental work. Although support exists for this expansion of responsibilities for dental health aide therapists, including among dental hygienists, the American Dental Association (ADA) is opposed, because of concerns that dental health aide therapists could be performing dental work in Alaska that would not be up to the standards of care offered to everyone else, and concerns that a CHAP dental health aide therapist program may be extended to the lower 48 states. The ADA argues that because of severe oral disease in the Alaskan Native population, highly skilled and trained dentists are needed to solve these dental challenges. Supporters of the dental health aide therapist program, on the other hand, claim that the need is so great that specially trained dental therapists could assist and solve many of the dental problems faced by remote villages. Currently, Alaska CHAP dental health aide therapists receive training outside the United States, because there are no U.S. programs training such dental health aide therapists.

Both bills would allow the CHAP dental health aide therapist program in Alaska to continue, but would prohibit any CHAP dental health aide therapists outside Alaska. H.R. 5312 (as introduced) would require that no CHAP certifications be granted to dental health aide therapists trained outside the United States if equivalent training were available inside the U.S. Both bills would also require a study of the Alaska CHAP dental health aide therapist program, to be conducted by a neutral panel of "clinicians, economists, community practitioners, oral epidemiologists, and Alaska Natives" (§121(c)(1)(B)), who would determine whether dental health aide therapist services are of adequate and appropriate quality and report to Congress and the HHS Secretary.

Health Services

In current law, the health services title (Title II) authorizes a number of specific health programs. In the bills Title II authorizes specific physical, but not mental, health programs. Programs are moved in from other titles, new programs are created, and a number of programs are moved to other titles; for instance, most of the mental health provisions of this title in current law are moved to the bills' "behavioral health" title (Title VII), and provisions on third-party reimbursements and managed care are moved to Title IV, which covers Medicare, Medicaid, and other programs (see discussions below).

The provisions that remain in the health services title broaden the range of health care services that the IHCIA authorizes IHS to provide. They add new authority for the Secretary to fund hospice care and long-term care for Indians. They update the Indian Health Care Improvement Fund to expand health services to Indians. They also set out the requirements for the Catastrophic Health Emergency Fund, including a new single-value threshold cost ($19,000) for treatment of victims. In addition, these provisions expand who can be billed for services under the SSA's Medicare, Medicaid, and SCHIP programs and allow broader purchase of insurance coverage. They broaden the provisions on diabetes prevention, treatment, and control; require that IHS establish an epidemiological center in every IHS service area; create an IHS Office of Indian Men's Health; and add oral health and youth programs to Indian school health education programs. They enlarge and combine the contract health service delivery areas (CHSDAs) in North and South Dakota to become one CHSDA covering both states. The provisions also allow health professionals licensed in any state, if employed by a THP, to provide services in any state served by that THP.

Diabetes

The bills replace the existing diabetes provision with new language that would require that IHS screen each eligible AI/AN for diabetes, determine the prevalence of and the types of complications of this disease, and take measures to reduce diabetes incidence. Language also requires the Secretary to continue funding all effective model diabetes prevention programs in existence on the date of enactment, as well as to establish dialysis programs, including purchasing equipment and providing necessary staffing. In addition, if funding is available, the Secretary is required to consult with THPs in each IHS area to establish a registry of diabetics in order to track the incidence and complications of diabetes in the area and further to ensure that the data are disseminated among all other area offices. The IHS could also establish a diabetes control officer in each IHS area office. The bills would also authorize IHS to establish criteria under which urban Indian organizations could receive grant funding for the prevention, treatment, and control of diabetes.

Health and Sanitation Facilities

In current law, health and sanitation facilities are covered in Title III. In the bills, several programs are transferred into Title III from other titles and new programs are created. Among the new provisions are a requirement that the Secretary develop a priority system for health-care facility construction; a requirement (instead of a discretionary authorization) that the Secretary provide financial and technical assistance to tribes, TOs, and Indian communities to establish utility organizations to operate and maintain sanitation facilities; authority to use IHS sanitation-facilities funding to fund tribes' loans to construct sanitation facilities; authorization for short-term, emergency IHS assistance to tribes in the operation of sanitation facilities; a requirement for a feasibility study for a new health-facility construction loan fund for tribes and TOs; authority for THPs to set rents on staff quarters; and authority for IHS to accept funding for health care facility construction from federal, state, and non-governmental sources. Another new provision reduces the minimum service-population size for funding the construction or modernization of small ambulatory care facilities, and expands the exemption from these minimum-size requirements (from tribes or TOs on islands, under current law, to tribal or TO facilities that are on islands or on road systems that do not give direct access to inpatient hospitals).

HUD Sanitation

Both bills prohibit the use of IHS sanitation-facilities funding to provide sanitation facilities for new homes funded by the Department of Housing and Urban Development (HUD). Congress has included a similar prohibition in annual IHS appropriations acts since FY2003. The goal of this provision is for HUD to fund sanitation facilities for HUD-financed new homes, so that IHS funds can be used to provide sanitation upgrades or initial sanitation services to existing Indian homes and to homes built or improved by tribes, the BIA, individuals, or other non-HUD public or private programs.

Negotiated Rulemaking

Title III of the bills greatly expands the application of negotiated rulemaking for IHS facilities. The Negotiated Rulemaking Act of 1990[68] created a process for making regulations in which the federal agency and representatives of interested groups (e.g., the group or industry to be regulated, community and public interest groups, or state or local governments) meet as a committee to reach consensus on a proposed regulation, before the proposal is published in the *Federal Register*. There are nine areas where the new Title III adds requirements for IHS to use negotiated rulemaking with tribes and TOs in promulgating relevant federal regulations: (1) establishing a priority system for health care facilities construction; (2) establishing construction standards for sanitation facilities; (3) evaluating needs for sanitation facilities; (4) applying Indian preference in construction or renovation of IHS facilities; (5) determining the methodology for the priority list for IHS funding to operate health facilities constructed by tribes with non-IHS funds; (6) approving applications for Indian health care delivery demonstration projects, unless the Secretary has promulgated regulations within one year of enactment of either bill; (7) establishing need criteria for tribal participation in the IHS-tribal facilities joint venture program; (8) setting the maximum renovation cost for health care facilities, above which a tribe may use maintenance and improvement funds to replace the facility; and (9) establishing health care facility construction standards. The facilities title is also covered by requirements for negotiated rulemaking in Section 802 of the bills (see discussion below).

Access to Health Services and Reimbursements

Authority for IHS health-care facilities to receive reimbursements from SSA's Medicare and Medicaid programs, contained in Title IV of current law, was a major component of the original IHCIA. The bills consolidate provisions covering reimbursements from third parties, whether from SSA programs or private parties, into Title IV. Several programs are moved in from other titles of current law, especially from the health services and miscellaneous provisions titles (Titles II and VIII, respectively), and new provisions are added.

A number of the provisions in Title IV, as well as related SSA provisions, continue to be negotiated among the relevant Senate and House committees and the Administration. S. 3524, the original bill reported by the Senate Finance Committee (which has jurisdiction over Medicaid, Medicare, and SCHIP), deals with these SSA health programs and many of the provisions in S. 1057 that amend or affect them, and is intended to be incorporated into S. 1057.

Several of the revised IHCIA provisions would change the status of tribes and TOs with regard to recovering funds under federal health care programs, in particular Medicare, Medicaid, and SCHIP (these programs are administered in HHS's Centers for Medicare and Medicaid Services, or CMS, and so are called

CMS programs). For example, Section 401(a) of S. 1057 adds SCHIP to existing IHCIA language excluding Medicare or Medicaid reimbursements from being considered when determining annual Indian health appropriations. Section 401(c) of S. 1057 continues the authority for a special fund for CMS reimbursement payments for services provided by IHS service units, but broadens the allowable uses and increases the proportion from 80% to 100% of the reimbursement that must go to the service unit that provided the health services, eliminating cost sharing for medical benefits. Section 401(d) of S. 1057 provides a new grant of direct authority for THPs to directly bill and receive reimbursement for prescribed services provided to eligible participants in all CMS programs, replacing a provision that only authorizes the Secretary to allow such direct billing (and only covers Medicare and Medicaid). Section 410 of S. 1057 authorizes THPs and UIOs to participate in SCHIP, in addition to IHS, and sets certain conditions. Additional changes regarding CMS programs are discussed below.

Payor of Last Resort

If an Indian is eligible for health care services under any other federal or state program, the IHS is authorized to enroll that Indian in the program and collect for that Indian's health service. When all other sources of payment are applied (including Medicaid, Medicare, SCHIP, any state program, or any private insurance), then IHS pays for the services not covered by those programs. Under a regulation in the current *Code of Federal Regulations*, IHS is designated as the payor of last resort, but only for contract health services.[69] Section 407 of the bills places the "payor of last resort" designation in statute and expands it to cover all services provided by an IHP or UIO.

Exemption from State or Local Licensing

All three bills exempt entities operated by the IHS, tribes, TOs, and UIOs from having to be licensed or recognized under state or local laws as a condition for eligibility for reimbursement from any federally-funded health program. Instead, such an entity shall be deemed to have met such state or local licensing requirements if it is determined that the entity "meets all applicable standards for such licensure." If any staff member of the entity lacks a state or local license, that fact may not be taken into account; S. 3524 and H.R. 5312, but not S. 1057, add that this provision applies only if the staff member has a valid license from another state. S. 3524 adds a prohibition on CMS payments to entities or individuals who have been excluded from participation in any federal health care program or whose license is under suspension or has been revoked by the state. S. 1057 puts the provision in IHCIA, while S. 3524 places it in the SSA. The bills do not state who determines that an entity meets all the applicable standards, and places no limits on the number or proportion of entity staffers who may not have state or local licenses.

Required Medicaid Consultations

All three bills require the Secretary to maintain an existing national advisory group to advise the Secretary on the need for the Secretary to consult with tribes, TOs, and UIOs on issues regarding CMS programs that would have implications for the IHP. No other state or entity has such access given by statute. S. 1057 places the provision in the IHCIA, while S. 3524 and H.R. 5312 (as ordered reported) place it in the SSA. Further, S. 3524 and H.R. 5312 require, while S. 1057 authorizes, a state receiving Medicaid payments to establish a consultation process with IHPs and UIOs that provide health care for which Medicaid assistance is available within that state. The state should consult regularly with these federal and Indian entities, especially before it submits any Medicaid plan amendments, waiver requests, or proposals for demonstration projects that are likely to have a direct effect on Indians, IHPs, or UIOs.

Exemptions from Various SSA Charges and Payments

Section 412 of S. 1057 exempts Indians from deductibles, co-payments, coinsurance payments, premiums, or enrollment fees under Medicaid or SCHIP. No means test is required. S. 3524 and H.R. 5312, as ordered reported, narrowed this exemption by limiting it to items and services provided by (or on a referral by) IHS, a tribe, TO, or UIO. These two bills also move the exemption from the IHCIA to the SSA. The Congressional Budget Office reports on S. 1057, S. 3524, and H.R. 5312 (as ordered reported) estimated that S. 1057's provisions would increase Medicaid and SCHIP spending by $26 million in FY2007 and by $357 million over the period FY2007-FY2016,[70] but that the narrower exemption in S. 3524 and H.R. 5312 would increase spending by only $6 million in FY2007 and $112 million over FY2007-2016.[71]

Exclusion of Property from Medicaid Eligibility Determinations

Section 412(c) of S. 1057 excludes certain Indian property from being considered in determining Medicaid eligibility. S. 3524 and H.R. 5312 (as ordered reported) include a very similar provision but move it from the IHCIA to the SSA. Property that must be excluded in defining eligibility includes all real property and improvements, whether in trust or not, located within Indian reservations and allotments, former reservations in Oklahoma (which may cover almost all of the state except the Panhandle and perhaps certain lands in southwestern Oklahoma), and Alaska Native regions established under the Alaska Native Claims Settlement Act[72] (which cover all of Alaska). Also excluded are ownership interests in income from natural-resource properties when the income results from exercising federally-protected rights. A further exclusion covers other property that is of "unique religious, spiritual, traditional, or cultural significance" or that is used for subsistence or to support a traditional lifestyle, according to tribal law or custom.

State Agreement to Indian Medicaid Managed Care Organization

All three bills add new Medicaid and SCHIP rules for managed care organizations concerning Indian enrollees, Indian health care providers, and Indian Medicaid managed care entities. They require that a state offer to make agreements to allow IHS, a tribe, a TO, or a UIO to serve as a Medicaid managed care organization, if (1) the state has elected to provide Medicaid services through managed care organizations and (2) an Indian Health Program or UIO, funded wholly or partly by IHS, has established a Medicaid managed care organization that meets the relevant required quality standards. S. 1057 adds these provisions to the IHCIA, while S. 3524 and H.R. 5312 (as ordered reported) place them in Section 1932 of the SSA.

Feasibility Study of Treating the Navajo Nation as a State under Medicaid and SCHIP

Section 414 of S. 1057 requires the Secretary to study the feasibility of allowing the Navajo Nation — a tribe with significant reservation land and population in three states (Arizona, New Mexico, and Utah) — to be treated as a state for the purposes of Medicaid and SCHIP services for all Indians within its boundaries. The study would assess whether an entity should be established to which, like a state Medicaid agency, the Secretary could pay all Medicaid, SCHIP, and related administrative expenditures that would ordinarily go to the states of Arizona, New Mexico, and Utah for Indians living within Navajo boundaries.

Annual Report on Indian CMS Beneficiaries

S. 3524, but not S. 1057, requires the Secretary, acting through CMS and IHS, to report annually to Congress on the enrollment and health status of Indians receiving SSA health care services or items during the previous year. Among the subjects to be covered would be Indians who receive benefits from both CMS and IHS, and the status of IHP and UIO facilities' compliance with CMS conditions and requirements.

Urban Indian Health Services

In current law, IHS funding for urban Indian health programs is authorized in Title V. The same title in the bills contains new and more inclusive programs for urban Indians and establishes a Division of Urban Indian Health in IHS. It adds several new programs and greatly revises others. Section 515 of S. 1057 grants UIOs the protections of the Federal Tort Claims Act;[73] H.R. 5312 has no similar provision. Section 517(a) of S. 1057 (§516(a) of H.R. 5312) expands the authorization for UIOs to use HHS federal facilities to include equipment and other personal property in the facilities. Under Section 517(e) of S. 1057 (§516(e) of H.R. 5312), UIOs carrying out IHS contracts or agreements would have access to federal vendors and suppliers on the same basis as federal executive agencies. Section 514 of the bills requires that IHS consult with UIOs "to the greatest extent practicable." Section 502 allows a UIO to provide health care services in any urban center, instead of just the urban center where the UIO is located. S. 1057's Section 516 (§515 of H.R. 5312) authorizes HHS funding for the construction and operation of at least two residential treatment centers in each state, for urban Indian youth who need culturally competent alcohol and substance abuse treatment services. S. 1057's Section 518 (§517 of H.R. 5312) authorizes grants to UIOs for diabetes prevention, treatment, and control, similar to existing diabetes grants to tribes and TOs (see §204 in the bills). Under Section 519/Section 518, UIOs are given access to the Community Health Representatives program (see §109 in the bills). Section 509 of both bills authorizes HHS to study the feasibility of federal direct or guaranteed loans for UIO facilities construction. Section 520/Section 519 makes all changes effective immediately upon enactment, whether any implementing regulations have been promulgated or not.

IHS Organizational Changes

The bills make no change in IHS's organizational status as a part of the Public Health Service within HHS, but do establish a new position of Assistant Secretary of Indian Health. They also authorize contracts and agreements with federal and state agencies and private and nonprofit organizations for enhancing information technology and add requirements that the automated management information system include a training component and an interface mechanism for the patient billing and accounts receivable system.

Elevation of the Director

Section 601 of the bills elevates the Director of IHS to the new position of Assistant Secretary of Indian Health under the Secretary of Health and Human Services. The new assistant secretary would be responsible for reporting to the

Secretary on all policy and budget matters relating to Indian health, coordinating department activities on Indian health matters, advising on all Indian health matters, and representing Indian issues to the heads of other HHS agencies and programs.

Behavioral Health Programs

Current law has a title (Title VII) covering alcohol and substance abuse programs. The bills expand the existing title to cover all mental and behavioral health programs, not just substance abuse. The aim is to create a "comprehensive behavioral health prevention and treatment program" (see §§701 and 703 in the bills). Title VII in the bills brings together all the mental and behavioral health programs that are in other titles of current law, generally substitutes the term "behavioral health" for the terms "mental health" and "alcohol and substance abuse," expands eligibility and additional practices, and adds numerous mandates to consult with tribes and TOs on policy decisions.

Section 709 of the bills authorizes HHS to provide one inpatient mental health care facility in each IHS service area (with California being divided into two areas). For Indian youth programs, Section 707 expands the existing alcohol and substance abuse program to cover all behavioral health problems. H.R. 5312 adds a provision to Section 707 authorizing grants to tribes, TOs, and UIOs for "Systems of Care" involving Indian families and communities in behavioral health services that address Indian youth suicide and other behavioral health needs. Other sections of the revised Title VII expand the program for community education and involvement on behavioral health issues to allow tribal and TO implementation (§710); change the fetal alcohol disorder (FAD) program to add diagnostic clinics, early intervention projects, and FAD housing (§712); add a youth telemental health demonstration project targeting Indian youth suicide (§708); and change the behavioral health research program by making tribes, TOs, and UIOs, instead of the IHS, the contractors with research institutions and by expanding the research program's subjects to include off-reservation, non-urban Indians receiving services (§714).

Other Issues

In current law, a number of separate provisions covering reports, regulations, and a variety of other topics are included in a "Miscellaneous" title (Title VIII). The bills retain this title, but add a number of new programs and move many provisions of current law to other titles.

Reports

Many titles of current law contain requirements for annual or onetime reports to Congress. Section 801 of current law requires additional reports and directs that most of the reports be transmitted to Congress with the President's annual submission of the U.S. government budget. The bills retain this pattern, but add a report comparing actual appropriations with amounts needed to achieve Indian parity with the general population in health status and services, and expand the required report on the impact of new national health-care programs to cover HHS consultation with TOs and UIOs.

Negotiated Rulemaking for Regulations

The bills greatly increase the number of instances where IHS must conduct negotiated rulemaking to create programs' regulations. The general requirement now (in §802 of current law) is that IHS must first consult with tribes and TOs and must publish final regulations in the *Federal Register* at least 60 days prior to their effective date. The new §802 in the bills would change the general authorization of regulations for IHCIA to (1) require negotiated rulemaking for regulations to carry out all provisions relating to human resources, health services, facilities, and behavioral health (Titles I (except §§105, 115, and 117), II, III (discussed above), and VII); (2) allow discretionary Administrative Procedure Act[74] rulemaking for certain Indian recruitment programs, reimbursements, and urban Indian health (§§105, 115, and 117 and Titles IV and V); and (3) prohibit rulemaking on IHS organization (Title VI) and for the miscellaneous-provisions title (Title VIII). Section 802 would also set a deadline for publication of all proposed regulations and a minimum time length for comment periods, and would create a final deadline of 24 months, after which rulemaking authority will expire.

Entitlement or Non-Entitlement[75]

The IHS health care delivery program is not an entitlement under federal law. IHS cannot commit funding for services if that funding has not been appropriated. Consequently, IHS health services depend each year on the annual appropriation. An entitlement program, on the other hand, such as Medicaid and Medicare, legally obligates the federal government to make payments to any person who meets the legal criteria for eligibility. An entitlement program may be funded through either permanent or annual appropriations, but the program's law requires that Congress appropriate whatever funds are needed. One of the major issues addressed in the IHCIA reauthorization bills before Congress is the tension between (1) the choices that must be made under the constraints of a finite annual appropriation and (2) the view of many Indians that their health care services are (or should be) an entitlement and, as such, are the sole responsibility of the federal government under trust or treaty obligations.

The advantage of an entitlement program for AI/AN would be that federal spending on eligible Indians' health care would not be limited to a specific appropriated amount. Spending controls on entitlement programs are done either by reducing benefits, limiting the health conditions covered, changing the eligibility requirements for beneficiaries, or generating new revenues. Among other issues that would have to be considered is the measure to be used to determine the entitlement's level of spending (e.g., a per capita Medicaid level). Proponents argue that AI/AN's loss of land and resources justifies making Indian health care an entitlement program. Some proponents are concerned about how a "beneficiary" would be defined, and whether Congress would require "means testing" as part of the eligibility criteria. These proponents argue that if Congress imposed "means testing", those AI/AN not meeting the means test would have their treaty rights abrogated. Opponents sometimes argue that federal Indian treaties and agreements did not promise unlimited health care services to all Indians or that Indians have already been compensated for lost lands and resources. Other opponents question whether an entitlement's "benefit package" would cover the non-clinical services (e.g., sanitation facilities) provided now through IHS. If non-clinical services were not provided, some believe that the quality of care would diminish under an entitlement program.

The bills would establish a national bi-partisan commission on Indian health care. The commission authorized by the 108th Congress bills would have been focused entirely on Indian health care entitlement and would have made recommendations as to whether health services could be provided to AI/AN under an entitlement program. The commission authorized under the bills in the 109th Congress would make recommendations on Indian health care delivery and related issues, including "the optimal manner" — such as entitlement — in which to provide Indian health care.

Eligibility for Services

Section 811 of the bills adds to IHCIA a provision postponing the application of a 1987 IHS regulation on health services eligibility until new eligibility criteria are developed through negotiated rulemaking (application of the regulation has been continually postponed in annual appropriations acts). (See "Eligible Population" above.)

Labor Law Exemption

Section 812 of the bills extends to those tribes and TOs carrying out self-determination contracts or self-governance compacts the same exemptions from the National Labor Relations Act[76] that federal, state, and local governments enjoy. Section 812 does not limit the application of this exemption to contracts or compacts with IHS or HHS, so it may apply to such contracts and compacts with all federal agencies.

Amendments to the Social Security Act

Separate from its reauthorization of IHCIA, S. 1057 amends Sections 1911 and 1932 (Medicaid) and Sections 2105 and 2107 (SCHIP) of the Social Security Act.[77] As noted above ("Access to Health Services and Reimbursements"), S. 3524 moves many provisions from the IHCIA to the SSA, as well as amending the same SSA sections as S. 1057.

SSA, Section 1880, which was added to that act by the 1976 IHCIA, makes IHS facilities, whether operated by IHS, a tribe or a TO, eligible for reimbursement from Medicare for coverable services. S. 1057 makes no changes in this section, but S. 3524 amends it to include UIOs and limit the services to those provided by IHS, a tribe, a TO, or a UIO. S. 3524 also amends SSA to require that IHS, tribal, TO, and UIO facilities who are not in compliance with CMS requirements not only make a plan to meet such requirements (as current law requires) — in order to be deemed in compliance during a 12-month grace period — but also make improvements in accordance with the plan.

SSA, Section 1911, also added to that act by the 1976 IHCIA, makes IHS, tribal, and TO facilities eligible for reimbursement from Medicaid for coverable services, and also authorizes HHS to make agreements to reimburse states for Medicaid-eligible services provided by IHS facilities. The bills amend SSA section 1911 to extend Medicaid eligibility to UIOs and to change eligibility from IHS *facilities* to the IHS, tribes, TOs, and UIOs as *organizations*, which appears to broaden the range of health services covered. The amendments to Section 1911 of SSA also require reimbursements for benefits covered under a state Medicaid waiver as well as under a state plan, and they also amend the current provision concerning reimbursements to states to specify that health services may be covered whether the delivery of the services is direct, through referral, or under contract or other arrangements.

S. 1057 amends SSA, Section 1932, which sets rules for states' use of managed care in Medicaid, to direct states using Medicaid managed care organizations to comply with Section 413 of S. 1057's IHCIA (as amended by S. 1057). S. 3524 and H.R. 5312 (as ordered reported) directly amend Section 1932 of SSA (see "State Agreement to Indian Medicaid Managed Care Organization" above).

Currently, SSA, Section 2105, allows SCHIP funds to be used to reimburse the IHS for care delivered to children eligible for both IHS services and SCHIP.[78] The bills amend current law to extend this SCHIP provision to tribes, TOs, and UIOs, as well as the IHS.

Other Legislative Issues

Congress has also considered other legislative initiatives that have a direct impact on Indian health.

Contract Support Costs

Under the Indian Self-Determination and Education Assistance Act (ISDEAA), IHS pays annual contract support costs to a tribe to cover the tribe's expenses for administering IHS programs under a self-determination contract (ISDEAA, Title I) or a self-governance compact (ISDEAA, Title III). Contract support costs are separate from direct program operating costs. They include pre-award costs (such as planning), one-time start-up costs (such as office-equipment purchases), direct costs (such as unemployment taxes on program salaries or training required for program personnel certification), and indirect costs (overhead costs shared with other programs, such as financial management, data processing, utilities, and janitorial services).[79] The amount of each tribe's contract support costs for IHS programs is negotiated between the tribe and IHS. The ISDEAA, however, makes the funding of contract support costs dependent on "the availability of appropriations."[80]

Funding, however, has been insufficient to cover tribal contract support costs. While appropriations for IHS contract support costs have risen over time (see Table 4 above), they have seldom covered 100% of the total contract support costs negotiated with tribes.[81] Moreover, the expenses that contract support costs are to pay have also gone up, because more tribes are electing to operate health delivery services, the total amount of program dollars contracted by the tribes has increased, and administrative costs have risen.[82]

When tribes' contract support costs are not fully funded through appropriations, the tribes must use program funds to make up the difference or else forego the administrative support. Contracting and compacting tribes argue that usage of program funds for contract support costs means less health treatment can be offered at IHS-funded centers. They have argued further that federal failure to pay contract support costs is a breach of federal contract law. The Cherokee Nation of Oklahoma and the Duck Valley Shoshone-Paiute Tribes of Nevada filed suits against the United States in the late 1990s, over IHS failure to fully fund the tribe's contract support costs, and eventually won their case before the U.S. Supreme Court.[83]

The tribes' victory in court does not appear, however, to fix the problem of the underfunding of contract support costs. The Supreme Court noted that the entire IHS appropriation from which contract support costs are drawn is available to pay the costs, but only if the appropriations act does not cap the amount appropriated for contract support costs.[84] Even before the Court decision, however, from FY1998 on, Congress began including language in appropriation acts that explicitly limited amounts for IHS contract support costs.

Besides increasing the appropriations, the main proposals for fully funding contract support costs involve making them an entitlement. Bills introduced in the 106th and 108th Congresses (H.R. 4148 and S. 2172, respectively) would both have made these costs an entitlement for IHS and BIA contracts and compacts. Neither bill was enacted. Proponents argued that contracting and compacting tribes are operating federal programs and carrying out federal responsibilities and that tribes should not have to use tribal financial resources to subsidize federal contract support costs.[85] Critics warned the proposal would be extremely expensive and argued that making an entitlement for one IHS funding source would jeopardize funding for other programs.

Substance Abuse and Mental Health Program Consolidation

Legislation was introduced in the 106th-108th Congresses to allow Indian tribes or TOs operating federal substance abuse and mental health programs to consolidate them into a single program for administrative purposes. AI/AN communities are increasingly plagued by mental health problems and alcohol and substance abuse at rates far greater than that of the general population. Alcohol continues to be an important risk factor associated with the top three killers of AI/AN youth —accidents, suicide, and homicide.[86] In fact, in 2002, alcohol was the primary abuse substance over illicit drugs among all AI/AN.[87] Compared to the average American, AI/AN are six times more likely to die from alcoholism-related diseases or accidents.[88] According to a Senate Committee on Indian Affairs report, mental health and social problems are associated with more than one-third of the demands made on Indian health facilities for services.[89] Other reports state that although little evidence is available, the existing data suggest that AI/AN youth and adults suffer a disproportionate burden of mental health problems when compared with other ethnic and racial groups in the United States.[90]

Recognizing that there is significant co-morbidity of mental and substance abuse disorders, particularly alcohol abuse, the federal government offers several disparate and currently uncoordinated mental health and substance abuse prevention and treatment programs for which tribes and tribal health organizations are eligible to receive funding. However, according to the Senate Committee on Indian Affairs report mentioned above, the funding available for the operation of these programs is generally very small.[91] Even in those instances where Indian tribes and tribal organizations are able to access program funding from several different sources, the amounts are generally so meager and the auditing and reporting requirements so onerous, according to the Senate Committee report, that it is simply not cost effective to attempt to operate a program which combines multiple sources of available funding. The Committee report also stated that a HHS study identified those department programs that could be consolidated by tribes into a self-governance compact, or that would be useful to a self-governance compact, but could not be consolidated due to statutory restrictions.[92]

The new Title VII of IHCIA in the bills emphasizes coordination of behavioral health care, but does not authorize consolidation of federal program funding. Separate legislation may be introduced to authorize tribal consolidation of federal substance abuse and mental health funding, as it was in the three preceding Congresses.

APPENDIX A. BRIEF HISTORY OF INDIAN HEALTH SERVICES

From 1789 to 1849, the Department of War was charged by Congress with handling Indian affairs (1 Stat. 49), so early federal health services to Indians were most likely to be provided by military doctors and were probably chiefly to prevent the spread of infectious diseases. Congressional appropriations for the War Department in this period did not mention Indian health care. In addition to whatever the War Department spent, some of the funds the federal government provided to missionaries for educating Indians may have been used for medical care of Indian students.

The earliest statutory authorization (and appropriation) explicitly for federal Indian health care was the act of May 5, 1832 (4 Stat. 514), which authorized Indian agents to employ local or U.S. Army doctors to provide smallpox vaccinations to Indians, and appropriated $12,000 for the purpose. Additional appropriations for smallpox vaccinations were made in 1839 (5 Stat. 328), 1853 (10 Stat. 226), and annually from 1860 to 1915.

The earliest Indian treaty providing for health services was signed on September 15, 1832 (7 Stat. 370), with the Winnebago of Wisconsin; it included funding for two physicians for 27 years as part of the compensation for a land cession. Of the approximately 210 treaties made with Indian tribes after this 1832 treaty until 1871 (when Congress ended Indian treaty-making), about 44 treaties committed the federal government to provide the signatory tribe(s) a physician, a hospital, medicines, or vaccine, or some combination of these, usually for a delimited period of time.

After 1849, when Indian affairs were transferred from the War Department to the new Department of the Interior (9 Stat. 395), federal executive activities regarding Indian health care fell under civilian rather than military authority. As the placement of Indian tribes on reservations accelerated in the second half of the 19th century, the federal government gradually became aware of the need for medical care on reservations. As noted, Congress made annual appropriations for Indian vaccination against smallpox from 1860 to 1915. By the 1860s Congress was also making appropriations for doctors and medicine for some agencies, and the BIA was appointing physicians, although only at some agencies. The number of medical employees in BIA agencies and schools increased from at least 12 in 1865 to 86 in 1897. By 1884 BIA regulations specified physicians' responsibilities, and by 1888 there were four BIA hospitals.

Except for 1873-1877, however, BIA had no organized medical division. Critics and studies inside and outside the BIA pointed out the severity of health problems, especially tuberculosis, in Indian schools and reservations. Between 1900 and 1911, however, the number of BIA hospitals and sanatoria jumped from five to 50, and in 1908 the BIA appointed its first chief medical supervisor. In 1910 Congress enacted its first appropriation for *general* Indian medical needs (36 Stat. 271), as opposed to appropriations for specific reservations or diseases, for $40,000. By 1920 Congress had increased this overall Indian health appropriation to $375,000, and had also added appropriations specifically for hospital construction and operation and for general medical treatment of Indians (and, for a few years, "correction of sanitary defects in Indian homes").

In 1921, Congress passed the Snyder Act (P.L. 67-85), a general authorization of appropriations for Indian health services, without time or dollar limitations (see "Statutory Authority," above). Despite these actions and further appropriations increases, criticism of BIA health services continued, including suggestions to transfer BIA medical services to the Public Health Service (PHS). In 1926 a PHS surgeon was assigned to supervise the BIA medical division. In 1929 Congress authorized the Secretary of the Interior to permit state agents to inspect AI/AN health and education conditions and to enforce sanitation and quarantine regulations (P.L. 70-760), and in 1934, through the Johnson-O'Malley Act (P.L. 73-167), Congress gave the BIA authority to contract for medical services from states, local governments, and private organizations.

Indian health problems were still severe, however. In 1955, under authority of the Transfer Act of 1954 (P.L. 83-568), the BIA's Indian health programs were transferred to the PHS in the then-new Department of Health, Education and Welfare, now HHS (see "Statutory Authority"). Indian Health Service appropriations increased markedly after the transfer, and Indians' health status improved greatly in the next 20 years. It still lagged behind that of the American population, however, and in 1976 Congress enacted the Indian Health Care Improvement Act (P.L. 94-437), authorizing new programs and IHS access to Medicaid and Medicare funds (see "Statutory Authority"). A year earlier, Congress had enacted the Indian Self-Determination and Education Assistance Act (P.L. 93-638), whose authorization of self-determination contracts and, through amendments, self-governance compacts has led to tribal operation of a majority of IHS facilities.

Printed Sources

Kappler, Charles J., comp. *Indian Affairs: Laws and Treaties*, 7 vols. (Washington: GPO, 1904-[1979]).
Pfefferbaum, Betty, et al. "Learning How to Heal: An Analysis of the History, Policy, and Framework of Indian Health Care," *American Indian Law Review*, vol. 20, no. 2, 1995-1996, pp. 365-397.
Prucha, Francis Paul. *The Great Father: The United States Government and the American Indians* (Lincoln: University of Nebraska Press, 1984).
Schmeckebier, Laurence F. *The Office of Indian Affairs: Its History, Activities, and Organization* (Baltimore: Johns Hopkins Press, 1927).
Stuart, Paul. *The Indian Office: Growth and Development of an American Institution, 1865-1900* (Ann Arbor, MI: UMI Research Press, 1978).
―― *Nations Within a Nation, Historical Statistics of American Indians* (New York, Greenwood Press, 1987).
United States, *United States Statutes At Large* (Boston: Little, Brown, 1851-1869, and Washington: GPO, 1875-present).

U.S. American Indian Policy Review Commission, Task Force Six: Indian Health, *Report on Indian Health. Final Report to the American Indian Policy Review Commission*, July 1976 (Washington: GPO, 1978).
U.S. Congress. House of Representatives. Committee on Energy and Commerce. Subcommittee on Health and the Environment. *Indian Health Care: An Overview of the Federal Government's Role*, 98th Cong., 2nd sess. H.Prt. 98-Y, April 1984 (Washington: GPO, 1984).

Online Sources

United States Statutes At Large, in the Library of Congress's American Memory site, "A Century of Lawmaking For a New Nation: U.S. Congressional Documents and Debates," at [http://memory.loc.gov/ammem/amlaw/lwsl.html].
Kappler's Indian Affairs: Laws and Treaties, at [http://digital.library.okstate.edu/kappler/].

REFERENCES

[1] Certain other AI/AN including urban Indians may be eligible for health services. (See later discussion on eligibility.)

[2] "The Congress hereby declares that it is the policy of the Nation, in fulfillment of its special responsibilities and legal obligations to the American Indian people, to meet the national goal of providing the highest possible health status to Indians and to provide existing Indian health services with all resources necessary to effect that policy" (§3, P.L. 94-437, act of Sept. 30, 1976, as amended; 25 U.S.C. 1602).

[3] Felix S. Cohen, *Handbook of Federal Indian Law* (1982 edition), Rennard Strickland, editor-in-chief (Charlottesville, VA: Michie Bobbs-Merrill, 1982), p. 677.

[4] See *Lincoln v. Vigil*, 508 U.S. 182, 194-195 (1993). This sentence was prepared by Nathan Brooks, Congressional Research Service Legislative Attorney, 2005.

[5] IHS service units are administrative entities within a defined geographical area through which services are directly or indirectly provided to eligible Indians. A service unit may cover a number of small reservations, or,

Indian Health Service: Health Care Delivery, Status, Funding... 43

conversely, some large reservations may be covered by several service units.
[6] As discussed below, the overall national area of contract health service delivery areas is identical to that of IHS service areas.
[7] ITU stands for: IHS-operated hospitals and clinics ("I"); the tribally-operated hospitals and clinics ("T"); and the urban Indian health organization programs ("U"). Ralph Forquera, *Issue Brief: Urban Indian Health* (Henry J. Kaiser Family Foundation, Nov. 2001), p. 8. [http://www.kff.org/minorityhealth/6006-index.cfm]. (Hereafter cited as Forquera, *Urban Indian Health*.)
[8] Contract health services are provided by non-IHS facilities or providers principally for members of tribes who live in contract health service delivery areas. 42 C.F.R. §136.23.
[9] Funding for UIHPs is authorized under §502 of the Indian Health Care Improvement Act (25 U.S.C. 1652), which directs the HHS Secretary to make grants to or contracts with UIHPs under the authority of the Snyder Act (25 U.S.C. 13). Such grants or contracts are not self-determination grants or contracts. See also Forquera, *Urban Indian Health*, pp. 12-13.
[10] P.L. 86-121, act of July 31, 1959, 73 Stat. 267; 42 U.S.C. 2004a.
[11] U.S. Indian Health Service, "Health and Heritage Brochure: Safe Water and Waste Disposal Facilities," available at [http://info.ihs.gov/Infrastructure/ 2_SafeWaterAnd Waste-Jan2005.doc], last accessed February 20, 2006.
[12] U.S. Department of Health and Human Services, Indian Health Service, *Justification of Estimates for Appropriations Committees, Fiscal Year 2007*, pp. IHF-9 — IHF-10.
[13] U.S. Department of Human Health and Services, Indian Health Service, Office of Public Health, *Level of Need Funded Study, LNF Workgroup Report II*, Dec. 1999, p. 2; available at [http://www.ihs.gov/ NonMedicalPrograms/Lnf/contP2Sum.htm].
[14] 42 C.F.R. §136.11(c).
[15] U.S. Indian Health Service, News Release, *Indian Health Service Receives 5% Funding Increase for FY2002*, Dec. 17, 2001; available at [http://www.ihs.gov/PublicInfo/ PublicAffairs/PressReleases/Press_Release_2001/Release_22_FY2002_IHS _Budget.asp].
[16] U.S. Congress, Senate Committee on Indian Affairs, *Partnership for a New Millennium: Addressing the Unmet Health Care Needs in Indian Country*, hearings, 105th Cong., 2nd sess., May 21, 1998 (Washington: GPO, 1998), pp. 15, 297. One article reported that, for example, in the Cherokee Nation

of Oklahoma, diabetics have had to be on the verge of losing a limb, a kidney, or their eyesight before the IHS health system covered their needed care. Katherine McIntire Peters, "The Long Wait," *Government Executive*, Dec. 2000, pp. 20-30; available at [http://www.govexec.com/features/1200/1200s1.htm].

[17] 42 C.F.R. §§136.11(c), 136.23(e).
[18] See [http://www.ihs.gov/GeneralWeb/HelpCenter/CustomerServices/approp.asp].
[19] U.S. Indian Health Service, "FY2006 Indian Health Service Budget Hearing: Questions for the Record: Additional Committee Questions," in U.S. Congress, House Committee on Appropriations, *Interior, Environment, and Related Agencies Appropriations for 2006*, hearings, part 6, 109th Cong., 1st sess. (Washington: GPO, 2005), pp. 278-279.
[20] 42 C.F.R. §136.12(a).
[21] "Terminated" tribes are tribes whose federal recognition was withdrawn by statute.
[22] 25 U.S.C. 1603(f), 1651 et seq.
[23] 25 U.S.C. 1680c: Health Services for Ineligible Persons.
[24] For instance, the act recognizing the Pascua Yaqui Tribe of Arizona set certain membership criteria (see §3, P.L. 95-375, act of Sept. 18, 1978, 92 Stat. 712; 25 U.S.C. 1300f-2), and an earlier act specified membership criteria for the Confederated Tribes and Bands of the Yakama Nation of Washington (§1, act of Aug. 9, 1946, Chap. 933, 60 Stat. 968; 25 U.S.C. 601).
[25] U.S. Department of Health and Human Services, Indian Health Service, *Trends in Indian Health, 2000-2001* (Washington: GPO, 2004), p. 33. Percentages calculated by CRS.
[26] Ibid., pp. 32-33.
[27] In the 2000 decennial census, respondents were for the first time permitted to identify themselves by more than one race.
[28] The census allows respondents to identify their tribe, but this is still self-identification. The census does not confirm a respondent's enrollment (or eligibility) in a federally-recognized tribe.
[29] U.S. Department of Health and Human Services, Indian Health Service, Office of Public Health, Division of Community and Environmental Health, Program Statistics Team, *Regional Differences in Indian Health, 1998-99* [Rockville, MD: IHS, (2000)], p. 11.

[30] U.S. Department of the Interior, Bureau of Indian Affairs, Office of Tribal Services, *Indian Labor Force Report, 1999* (Washington: BIA, n.d.), pp. I-iii.
[31] See 25 U.S.C. 1603(f), 1651 *et seq.*
[32] Forquera, *Urban Indian Health*, p. 1; and Appendix 1; and Marlita A. Reddy, ed., *Statistical Record of Native North Americans* (Detroit: Gale Research, 1993), p. 420.
[33] IHS, Trends in Indian Health, 2000-2001, p. 158.
[34] Diabetes is a disease in which the body either does not produce the hormone insulin (Type 1) or does not properly use insulin (Type 2). Insulin converts sugar, starches, and other foods into energy. About 90-95% of diabetics have Type 2 diabetes. See [http://www.diabetes.org/advocacy-and-legalresources/federal_legislation/overview.jsp].
[35] U.S. Department of Health and Human Services, Indian Health Service, *Justification of Estimates for Appropriations Committees, Fiscal Year 2007*, p. IHS-71.
[36] Ibid., p. 71.
[37] U.S. Commission on Civil Rights, *Broken Promises: Evaluating the Native American Health Care System* (Washington: The Commission, Sept. 2004), p. 10 n.20.
[38] U.S. Indian Health Service, National Diabetes Program, *Interim Report to Congress: Special Diabetes Program for Indians*, Dec. 2004, p. 161.
[39] Diabetes Prevention Program Research Group, "Reduction in the Incidence of Type 2 Diabetes with Lifestyle Intervention or Metformin," *The New England Journal of Medicine*, vol. 346, no. 6, Feb. 7, 2003, pp. 393-403.
[40] U.S. Department of Health and Human Services, National Institute of Diabetes and Digestive and Kidney Diseases, National Institute of Health, "National Diabetes Education Program Tailors Cardiovascular Disease Message for American Indians and Alaska Natives," *NIH News*, May 16, 2005.
[41] For information on IHS FY2007 appropriations, see CRS Report RL33399, *Interior, Environment, and Related Agencies: FY2007 Appropriations*, by Carol Hardy Vincent and Susan Boren.
[42] Current dollars were deflated to constant dollars using the Consumer Price Index for All Urban Consumers (CPI-U) for All Items. Different price indexes are used to deflate medical cost increases. IHS often uses the CPI-U for Medical Care. For this report CRS considered the CPI-U for All Items the most applicable price index.

[43] States receive 100% federal reimbursement for Medicaid services provided to eligible AI/ANs through IHS- and tribe-owned or -operated facilities.
[44] U.S. Indian Health Service, "FY2006 Indian Health Service Budget Hearing: Questions for the Record: Additional Committee Questions," in U.S. Congress, House Committee on Appropriations, *Interior, Environment, and Related Agencies Appropriations for 2006*, hearings, Part 6, 109th Cong., 1st sess. (Washington: GPO, 2005), p. 270.
[45] "Statement of Buford Rolin, Chairman, National Indian Health Board," in U.S. Congress, Senate Committee on Indian Affairs, *Partnership for a New Millennium* (1998), op. cit., pp. 279-280, 293. The IHS per capita figure is based on direct appropriations (including construction but excluding reimbursements) divided by the IHS service population. See also Jo Ann Kauffman, *Reauthorization of the Indian Health Care Improvement Act: Background and Issues* (Henry J. Kaiser Family Foundation. Oct. 1999), [http://www.kff. org/minorityhealth/loader.cfm?url=/ commonspot/security/getfile.cfm and PageID=13244].
[46] Calculated by CRS, in current dollars. Appropriations figure is from Table 2; population data are from *Trends in Indian Health 1998-99*, op. cit., p. 36.
[47] Annual medical costs per inmate, as calculated by BOP. U.S. Federal Bureau of Prisons, "1990-2000 Medical Per Capita Costs," unpublished table transmitted to CRS Feb. 2002.
[48] VA medical care obligations per unique patient, in current dollars; per-capita calculated by CRS. U.S. Department of Veterans Affairs, *FY2002 Budget Submission. Medical Programs*, vol. 2 of 6. Office of the Assistant Secretary for Financial Management, pp. 2-39, 2-42.
[49] See the FDI webpage at [http://www.ihs.gov/NonMedicalPrograms/ Lnf/index.htm]. The workgroup's latest report is: U.S. Department of Health and Human Services, Indian Health Service, *2001 IHCIF, Final Results for the FY 2001 Indian Health Care Improvement Fund*, Apr. 2001. See [http://www.ihs.gov/NonMedicalPrograms/ Lnf/conIHCIF.htm]. An earlier report was: U.S. Department of Health and Human Services, Indian Health Service, Office of Public Health, *Level of Need Funded Study, LNF Workgroup Report II*, Dec. 1999 [http://www.ihs.gov/NonMedical Programs/ Lnf/contP2Sum.htm].
[50] The Federal Employees Health Benefits Plan is the program under which all non-military federal employees obtain federal health coverage.
[51] For the figures cited in the preceding sentences, see [http://www.ihs.gov/ NonMedicalPrograms/Lnf/IHCIF2001/2001ConsolidatedReport.pdf],

especially table C, "February 13, 2001, letter of recommendations from the LNF Workgroup" and table 8b.

[52] U.S. Indian Health Service, "House Interior Appropriations, Committee Questions for the Record," in U.S. Congress, House Committee on Appropriations, *Department of the Interior and Related Agencies Appropriations for 2001*, hearings, part 8, 106th Cong., 2nd sess.

[53] U.S. Indian Health Service, personal communications, June 30 and July 1, 2005.

[54] Act of Nov. 2, 1921, 42 Stat. 208, as amended; 25 U.S.C. 13.

[55] P.L. 83-568, act of Aug. 5, 1954, 68 Stat. 674, as amended; 42 U.S.C. 2001 et seq.

[56] P.L. 86-121, act of July 31, 1959, 73 Stat. 267; 42 U.S.C. 2004a.

[57] P.L. 93-638, act of Jan. 4, 1975, 88 Stat. 2203, as amended; 25 U.S.C. 450 et seq.

[58] Title II of P.L. 100-472, act of Oct. 5, 1988, 102 Stat. 2285, 2296.

[59] §814 of P.L. 102-573, act of Oct. 29, 1992, 106 Stat. 4526, 4590.

[60] P.L. 106-260, act of Aug. 18, 2000, 114 Stat. 711; 25 U.S.C. 458aaa et seq.

[61] P.L. 94-437, act of Sept. 30, 1976, 90 Stat. 1400, as amended; 25 U.S.C. 1601 et seq., and 42 U.S.C. 1395qq, 1396j (and amending other sections).

[62] P.L. 106-417, act of Nov. 1, 2000, 114 Stat.1812; 25 U.S.C. 1601 note, 1645, and 42 U.S.C. 1395qq(e), 1396j(d).

[63] S. 1057 has five sections; one subsection (§2(a)) contains the reauthorization of IHCIA eight core titles, while §4 amends SSA provisions added or amended by the IHCIA.

[64] U.S. Congress, Senate Committee on Finance, *Medicare, Medicaid, and SCHIP Indian Health Care Improvement Act of 2006*, a report to accompany S. 3524, 109th Cong., 2nd sess., S.Rept. 109-278 (Washington: GPO, 2006), p. 1.

[65] Telephone conversation with an IHS spokesman, Nov. 4, 2004.

[66] Act of Apr. 30, 1908, Chap. 153 (60th Cong.), 35 Stat. 70, 71; §23 of the act of June 25, 1910, Chap. 431 (61st Cong.), 36 Stat. 855, 861, as amended; 25 U.S.C. 47.

[67] Eugene Sekiguchi, Albert H. Guay, L. Jackson Brown, and Thomas J. Spangler, Jr., "Improving the Oral Health of Alaska Natives," *American Journal of Public Health*, vol. 95, no. 5, May 2005, pp. 769-772.

[68] P.L. 101-648, act of Nov. 29, 1990, 104 Stat. 4970; 5 U.S.C., Chap. 5, Subchap. III.

[69] See 42 C.F.R. 136.61.

[70] U.S. Congressional Budget Office, "Cost Estimate: S. 1057, Indian Health Care Improvement Act Amendments of 2005, As Reported by the Senate Committee on Indian Affairs on March 16, 2006," April 26, 2006, pp. 5-6.
[71] U.S. Congressional Budget Office, "Cost Estimate: S. 3524, Medicare, Medicaid, and SCHIP Indian Health Care Improvement Act of 2006, As Reported by the Senate Committee on Finance on June 15, 2006," July 10, 2006, pp. 2-4; and U.S. Congressional Budget Office, "Cost Estimate: H.R. 5312, Indian Health Care Improvement Act Amendments of 2006, As Ordered Reported by the House Committee on Resources on June 21, 2006," July 28, 2006, pp. 3-4. H.R. 5312 has not been reported yet, but the CBO report on H.R. 5312 states that the bill's provisions affecting Medicaid and SCHIP spending are identical to those in S. 3524 (*ibid.*, p. 7).
[72] P.L. 92-203, Act of Dec. 18, 1971, 85 Stat. 688, as amended; 43 U.S.C., Chap. 33.
[73] Act of Aug. 2, 1946, Chap. 753 (79th Cong.), Title IV, 60 Stat. 842, as amended; 28 U.S.C., Chap. 171.
[74] Act of June 11, 1946, Chap. 324 (79th Cong.), 60 Stat. 237, as amended; 5 U.S.C., Chap. 5.
[75] Jo Ann Kauffman, *Reauthorization of the Indian Health Care Improvement Act: Background and Issues*. One of a series of papers commissioned by the Henry J. Kaiser Family Foundation, Oct. 1999.
[76] Act of July 5, 1935, Chap. 372 (74th Cong.), 49 Stat. 450, as amended; 29 U.S.C., Chap. 7, subchap. II.
[77] These SSA amendments are in §4 of S. 1057.
[78] Normally federal funds provided under SCHIP may not substitute for funding from other federal government programs — such as IHS — that would otherwise cover the costs of care delivered to SCHIP-enrolled children.
[79] U.S. General Accounting Office, *Indian Self-Determination Act: Shortfalls in Indian Contract Support Costs Need to Be Addressed*, Report to Congressional Requestors, GAO/RCED-99-150, June 1999, Washington, 1999. See table 1.1, p. 18.
[80] ISDEAA, §106(b); 25 U.S.C. 450j-1(b).
[81] GAO, Indian Self-Determination Act: Shortfalls in Indian Contract Support Costs, pp. 33-35.
[82] Ibid., p. 3.
[83] Cherokee Nation of Oklahoma v. Leavitt, 453 U.S. __, WL464860 (Mar. 1, 2005). For further analysis of this case, see CRS Report RL32681, Indian Self-Determination and Education Assistance Act Contracts and Cherokee

Nation of Oklahoma v. Leavitt: Agency Discretion to Fund Contract Support Costs, by Nathan Brooks.

[84] *Cherokee Nation of Oklahoma* v. *Leavitt*, 453 U.S. __, WL464860 (2005) (slip opinion at 4).

[85] U.S. Congress, House Committee on Resources, *Tribal Contract Support Cost Technical Amendments of 2000*, report to accompany H.R. 4148, 106th Cong., 2nd sess., H.Rept. 106-837 (Washington: GPO, 2000), p. 4.

[86] U.S. Congress, Senate Committee on Indian Affairs, To Authorize the Integration and Consolidation of Alcohol and Substance Abuse Programs and Services Provided by Indian Tribal Governments, and for Other Purposes, a report to accompany S. 285, 108th Cong., 1st sess., S.Rept. 108-75 (Washington: GPO, 2003), p. 2 (hereafter cited as Senate Committee on Indian Affairs, Alcohol and Substance Abuse Programs).

[87] U.S. Department of Health and Human Services, Substance Abuse and Mental Health Services Administration (SAMHSA),Office of Applied Studies, "The DASIS Report (Drug and Alcohol Services Information System)," Feb. 11, 2005, found at [http://www.oas.samhsa.gov/2k5/IndianTX/IndianTX.cfm].

[88] U.S. Congress, House Committee on Appropriations, Subcommittee on Interior, Environment, and Related Agencies, *FY2006 Indian Health Service Budget Hearing Questions for the Record*, hearings on Interior, Environment, and Related Agencies Appropriations for 2006, part 6, p. 269.

[89] Senate Committee on Indian Affairs, *Alcohol and Substance Abuse Programs*, p. 2.

[90] Department of Health and Human Services, U.S. Public Health Service, Substance Abuse and Mental Health Services Administration, Center for Mental Health Services, *Mental Health, Culture, Race, and Ethnicity, A Supplement to Mental Health: A Report of the Surgeon General*, Rockville, MD 2001, p. 96.

[91] Senate Committee on Indian Affairs, *Alcohol and Substance Abuse Programs*, p. 2.

[92] Ibid.

In: Native Americans: Rights, Laws...
Editor: C. P. Townsend, pp. 51-70

ISBN: 978-1-60456-202-6
© 2008 Nova Science Publishers, Inc.

Chapter 2

INDIAN RESERVED WATER RIGHTS: AN OVERVIEW[*]

Nathan Brooks

ABSTRACT

With the dramatic population increase in the West over the last thirty years, the Western states have been under increasing pressure from their citizens to secure future access to water. In planning to meet this goal, however, Western officials have had to confront a heretofore obscure doctrine of water law: the doctrine of Indian reserved water rights, also known as the *Winters* doctrine. This doctrine holds that when Congress reserves land for an Indian reservation, Congress also reserves water to fulfill the purpose of the reservation. When this doctrine is applied to the water laws of the Western states, tribal rights to water are almost always senior to other claimants. Therefore, in order for Western water officials to effectively plan for a stable allocation of water on which all parties can rely, they must find a way to satisfy the water claims of local Indian tribes. The parties originally took to the courts to resolve these issues, only to find themselves in an endless cycle of litigation that rarely produced definitive rulings. As a result, negotiated settlements - which require Congressional authorization in order to be valid - are fast becoming the norm. This report provides an overview of the legal issues surrounding Indian reserved water rights disputes.

---

[*] Excerpted from CRS Report RL32198, dated January 24, 2005.

INTRODUCTION

"When the well is dry," wrote Benjamin Franklin, "we learn the worth of water."[1] The people of the arid American West have always lived in fear of a dry well, and the dramatic increase in the Western population over the last century has brought with it a rise in the number of mouths clamoring for water.[2] Consequently, the drive to secure water often pits states, municipalities, and individual landowners against each other in epic political struggles. This drive also spurs planning and innovation as officials look for new technological means to deliver water from wherever it can be found. As a result, we have water projects like the Central Utah Project (CUP) and the massive Central Arizona Project (CAP).

In planning to ensure that their citizens have access to water in the future, Western states have had to confront a heretofore obscure doctrine of water law: the doctrine of Indian reserved water rights, also known as the *Winters* doctrine. This doctrine holds that when Congress reserves land for an Indian reservation, Congress also reserves water to fulfill the purpose of the reservation. When this doctrine is applied to the water laws of the Western states, tribal rights to water are almost always senior to other claimants. Therefore, in order for Western water officials to effectively plan for a stable allocation of water on which all parties can rely, they must find a way to satisfy the water claims of local Indian tribes.

Satisfying these claims has proven a difficult task, largely because the *Winters* doctrine offers very little guidance regarding just how much water the tribes are entitled to. The effort started with litigation but, as this chapter will discuss, judges have proven unable to fashion an effective method for balancing the literally thousands of interests in water rights adjudications. Increasingly, then, these disputes have moved from the courtroom to the negotiating table, and settlements are fast becoming the norm.[3] Because of the federal government's unique role with respect to Indian tribes, Congress must ratify these settlement agreements in order for them to be valid. As more and more of these settlements come to Congress for approval,

it is important for legislators to have an understanding of the *Winters* doctrine and the very complicated legal issues surrounding it.

Winters and the Reserved Water Rights Doctrine

The Western states all determine water rights using some form of the prior appropriation doctrine, which holds that rights to water belong to the party that first puts the water to "beneficial use."[4] As long as the party continues to put that water to beneficial use, its prior appropriation right remains senior to all other users.[5] Many commentators condense the entire doctrine, somewhat glibly, into six words: first in time, first in right.

In 1908, the Supreme Court added a complicated twist to this system when it promulgated what came to be known as the reserved rights doctrine in *Winters v. United States*.[6] There, the Court ruled that when Congress set aside land for the Fort Belknap Indian Reservation, Congress also impliedly reserved water to help transform the tribe into a "pastoral and civilized people."[7] It is important to stress here that the Court reached this conclusion not by looking to the Constitution or explicit statutory language, but rather by *implying* a certain Congressional intent. To this day, the *Winters* doctrine remains such an implication.

The Supreme Court has continued to imply the same Congressional intent with regard to all federal reservations - tribal or otherwise (e.g., national parks) - stating that "when the Federal Government withdraws its land from the public domain and reserves it for a federal purpose, the Government, by implication, reserves appurtenant water then unappropriated to the extent needed to accomplish the purpose of the reservation."[8] The amount must satisfy both present and future needs of the reservation.[9] This reserved water right vests on the date that Congress reserves the land,[10] and remains regardless of non-use.[11] Therefore, because most Indian reservations were created in the 1800's or early 1900's, such reservations are generally both first in time and first in right under the Western prior appropriation system.[12]

While *Winters* established a reserved water right for Indian reservations, for most of the last century that right amounted to nothing more than "paper water,"[13] as many took to calling it, because without either a standard for quantifying that right or the technological means to take advantage of it, Indian tribes had little hope of seeing a drop of actual (i.e., "wet") water. To remedy this situation, the tribes were forced to seek assistance from the United States government, which holds most reservation property in trust for the Indian tribes. Congress has charged the Interior and Justice Departments with many of its responsibilities as trustee to advance the water rights of the Indian tribes.[14] However, these departments are also charged with advancing the broader national interest in water use, creating a conflict of interest which, until relatively recently, almost always weighed in favor of non-Indian interests, and against the development of tribal water projects.[15] While under normal fiduciary principles such a conflict would not be tolerated, the Supreme Court has recognized that the United States in its unique relationship with Indian tribes cannot be held to the same standards as a private trustee. As the Court put it in a water rights case involving a conflict in legal representation,

> It may well appear that Congress was requiring the Secretary of the Interior to carry water on at least two shoulders when it delegated to him both the responsibility for the supervision of the Indian tribes and the commencement of reclamation projects in areas adjacent to reservation lands. But Congress chose to do this...the Government cannot follow the fastidious standards of a private fiduciary, who would breach his duties to his single beneficiary solely by representing potentially conflicting interests without the beneficiary's consent.[16]

With the population increasing in the West and the resulting need to secure access to water, Westerners were forced to deal with the senior claims of the tribes holding reserved water rights. Against this backdrop, various state, local, and tribal claimants to water have filled the courts for decades in order to settle the myriad of issues left open by the Supreme Court in *Winters*. In the process, the question of which courts possess the power to resolve these issues has been almost as contentious as the issues themselves.

THE MCCARRAN AMENDMENT

For most of the last century, the doctrine of sovereign immunity shielded tribes and the federal government from state water rights adjudications, and so federal courts had near-exclusive power to determine *Winters* rights.[17] In 1952, however, Congress passed an appropriations rider waiving the federal government's sovereign immunity and permitting joinder of the United States in suits involving the adjudication of water rights of a river system or other source.[18] Known today as the McCarran Amendment, the law provides for consent to join the United States "in any suit (1) for the adjudication of rights to the use of water of a river system or other source, or (2) the administration of such rights, where it appears that the United States is the owner of, or is in the process of acquiring water rights under State law, by purchase, by exchange, or otherwise, and the United States is a necessary party to such suit."[19] In a momentous 1976 decision, the Supreme Court held that the McCarran Amendment allows state courts to adjudicate Indian water rights where the United States is sued in its role as trustee for the tribes.[20] For Indian tribes that have long considered state courts to be hostile territory, the prospect of having those same courts adjudicate

Indian water rights has been one of the primary motivations for pursuing negotiated settlements.[21]

In its decision allowing state court adjudications of tribal water rights under the McCarran Amendment, the Supreme Court held that the policy behind the amendment - namely, the avoidance of piecemeal adjudication of water rights in a river system - requires that state court adjudications under the McCarran Amendment must be "comprehensive" in order to be valid. As the Court put it, "The consent to jurisdiction given by the McCarran Amendment bespeaks a policy that recognizes the availability of comprehensive state systems for adjudication of water rights."[22] Factors that contribute to a particular adjudication's "comprehensiveness" include the parties, the types of rights at issue, the definition of the basin to be included in the adjudication, and the time frame covered by the adjudication.[23]

While the law is clear that the McCarran Amendment grants state courts the right to adjudicate Indian water rights, the question of who has the power to *administer* water rights determined in a McCarran Amendment adjudication is not so clear.[24] Some argue that the above-quoted language of the McCarran Amendment distinguishing between administration and adjudication of water rights is meant to limit a state's ability to administer such rights.[25] The Wyoming Supreme Court has held, though, that state courts have the power to administer as well as adjudicate Indian water rights.[26] Significantly, the court also ruled that an appointed State Engineer has the power to "monitor" water use under a court's reserved rights decree, but enforcement by that same official against either the tribes or the United States would require judicial action.[27]

The benefit of the McCarran Amendment is that it allows a state to take a more active role in the determination of a resource so precious to all of that state's citizens. As discussed above, however, the Supreme Court in *Winters* left many questions regarding reserved water rights to be determined by other courts. In the wake of the McCarran Amendment, most of the courts to take up these questions have been various state judicial bodies, with different states sometimes providing very different answers. This lack of uniformity breeds confusion, which is nowhere more evident than in the courts' handling of the quantification problem.

LITIGATION AND QUANTIFICATION

Using the *Winters* rationale to guide them in their search for a quantification standard, courts have generally focused first on each reservation's purpose, and then determined the amount of water necessary to fulfill that purpose. Until recently, virtually every court to consider the question of a reservation's purpose held that purpose to be agricultural, in that the federal government, in reserving the land, intended that the Indians who inhabited the reservation would cultivate the land in order to become self-sufficient.[28] Subsequent judicial attempts to establish a quantification standard in line with this agricultural purpose have resulted in some standards, but also more confusion.[29] While some courts followed the Supreme Court's lead in *Winters* and refused to establish a quantification standard,[30] other courts tried a "reasonable needs" approach that looked to past and present water use as a benchmark.[31]

The Supreme Court made its most significant contribution to the quantification debate in *Arizona v. California*, in which the Court expressed its approval of the Special Master's use of a fixed calculation of water needs based on the physical capacity of the reservation land, rather than the number of Indians on the reservation.[32] The Special Master based this "practicably irrigable acreage" (PIA) standard, as it has come to be known, on the aforementioned assumption that the purpose of an Indian reservation is agricultural. Starting from that assumption, the Special Master reasoned, and the Court agreed, that "the only feasible and fair way by which reserved water for the reservation can be measured is irrigable acreage."[33] Interestingly, while the Supreme Court endorsed the Special Master's use of the PIA standard in *Arizona*, the Court did not technically adopt it. As the Court put it, "While we have in the main agreed with the Master, there are some places we have disagreed and some questions on which we have not ruled. Rather than adopt the Master's decree...we will allow the parties, or any of them, if they wish, to submit...the form of decree to carry this opinion into effect."[34] This unusual set of facts has led many to question the precedential value of the Court's decision in *Arizona*.[35]

Notwithstanding the debate over *Arizona*'s precedential value, the PIA standard is today by far the favorite judicial method for quantifying Indian reserved water rights,[36] and lower courts have fashioned a three-step process for determining a reservation's practicably irrigable acreage.[37] First, soil scientists determine the largest area of arable land that can reasonably be considered for an irrigation project.[38] Second, engineers develop an irrigation system based on the available water supply and the arable land base.[39] Third, economists evaluate the crop patterns, yields, pricing, and the net returns for crops that the irrigation project might support.[40]

While the widespread judicial adoption of the PIA standard currently provides parties with some degree of certainty as to how Indian water rights will be quantified by courts, that standard is by no means set in stone, and there is evidence to suggest not only that courts may soon be moving away from the PIA standard, but also that they may be doing so in slightly different directions, adding to the uncertainty. First, non-Indian appropriators argue that agricultural water use is highly consumptive, and therefore the PIA standard is too friendly to Indians and insensitive to state and private appropriators.[41] There is evidence in Justice Thurgood Marshall's papers that before Justice O'Connor recused herself in *Wyoming v. United States*,[42] she authored a draft majority opinion in which the Court would have held that the quantification of Indian water rights must include a sensitivity analysis, taking into account the effect on other state and private appropriators.[43] Given how close the Supreme Court came to restructuring the PIA standard in *Wyoming*, it is possible that the Court might adopt a stricter standard in the future.

On the other side of the ideological spectrum, some argue that the PIA standard is not friendly enough to Indians, in that linking water rights to agriculture is anachronistic and unfair given the current state of the agricultural economy in this country.[44] Others contend that the PIA standard does not take into account the realities of modern-day life and the diversity of reservations' geographies and purposes.[45] Agreeing with both sides of the PIA debate in some respects, the Arizona Supreme Court in its 2002 *Gila River* ruling abandoned agriculture as the sole purpose for Indian reservations and found instead that the essential purpose of an Indian reservation is to establish a "permanent home and abiding place."[46] Citing various water settlements, the court found its construction necessary "to achieve the twin goals of Indian self-determination and economic self-sufficiency."[47] In quantifying water rights in line with that purpose, the court held as proper a reservation-by-reservation analysis of, among other things, (1) the tribe's history and culture; (2) the reservation's geography and natural resources, including groundwater availability; (3) the reservation's physical infrastructure, human resources, technology, and capital; (4) past water use; and (5) a tribe's present and projected future population.[48]

While the Arizona Supreme Court's approach addresses many of the criticisms leveled at the PIA standard, its "reservation-by-reservation" focus does not lend itself to a specific formula, and so could lead to more uncertainty for authorities trying to account for Indian reserved water rights when planning large water projects. Of course, the *Gila River* decision is only one case with no precedential value in other states. It is still too soon to tell whether or not the Arizona Supreme Court's *Gila River* ruling will spur other states to follow suit and reassess the PIA standard. What is clear, however, is that there are serious questions - from all sides - about the effectiveness of that standard.

WINTERS AND ALLOTTEE RIGHTS

While the task of quantifying *Winters* water often frustrates judges, adjudications involving *Winters* rights become even more confusing when allotments are involved. In an effort to assimilate Indians into mainstream American culture, Congress in 1887 passed the General Allotment Act[49] - also known as the Dawes Act - authorizing the President to allot portions of reservation lands to individual Indians. Title would then remain in the United States in trust for 25 years, after which it would pass to the individual Indian allottees free from all encumbrances.[50] The act also authorized the Secretary of the Interior to distribute surplus reservation land for the purpose of non-Indian settlement. After the 25-year trust period was over, many allottees found themselves unable to pay the state taxes to which their lands became subject, resulting in widespread forced sales.[51] These forced sales combined with the Secretary's distribution of surplus lands to non-Indians to produce a "checkerboard" pattern of Indian/non-Indian land ownership far different from what Congress intended in passing the Dawes Act.[52]

While many reservations escaped allotment and its consequences, this "checkerboard" pattern of ownership on some reservations persists and today presents serious problems in reserved water rights disputes. The Supreme Court ruled somewhat confusingly in the only allottee water rights case to come before it that when tribal land is converted into allotments, the allottees succeed to *some portion* of tribal waters needed for agriculture.[53] A subsequent Ninth Circuit case, *Colville Confederated Tribes v. Walton*, built on that reasoning and held that an allottee's share of a tribe's reserved water is equal to the percentage of the entire reservation's irrigable acreage that is located on the allottee's land.[54] The *Walton* court also found that a non-Indian successor in interest to an Indian allottee acquires that allotment's reserved water right, but loses that right if the non-Indian successor does not put the water to beneficial use.[55] The Supreme Court's ruling and the later lower court cases expanding on it considered allotment rights only for irrigation purposes. It is not clear how these holdings relate to reservations of land for nonagricultural purposes.

TRIBAL USE OF ITS RESERVED WATER RIGHT

As the *Gila River* decision discussed earlier illustrates, a court's answer to the threshold question of purpose can have far-reaching effects. The Arizona Supreme Court's finding of a "permanent homeland" purpose not only led the court to a new method of quantification, but also allowed the court to put a premium on flexibility in how tribes use their *Winters* water. As the court put it, "Just as [the U.S.] economy has evolved, nothing should prevent tribes from diversifying their economies if they so choose and are reasonably able to do so. The permanent homeland concept allows for this flexibility and practicality."[56] This is consistent with the opinion of the Special Master in *Arizona v. California*, who stated that, even though he found the reservation's purpose to be agricultural, that did not mean that the reserved water had to be put to agricultural use.[57]

The *Gila River* court specifically rejected the approach taken by the Wyoming Supreme Court ten years earlier in the *Big Horn* adjudication.[58] There, the court found that because agriculture was the primary purpose for the reservation of land for the Indians, if the tribe wanted to use the water for some other purpose, such as instream flow, the tribe must do so according to state prior appropriation doctrine.[59] In reaching its conclusion, the Wyoming Supreme Court relied on the primary-secondary purpose test used in *United States v. New Mexico*,[60] a Supreme Court case dealing with a non-Indian federal reservation, specifically a national forest. The Court in *New Mexico* found that the United States, in setting aside federal lands for the Gila National Forest, reserved use of the Rio Mimbre River only where necessary to preserve timber and to secure favorable water flows, and therefore did not have the reserved right for aesthetic, recreational, wildlife preservation, or stock watering purposes.[61] As the Court stated, "Where water is necessary to fulfill the very purposes for which a federal reservation was created, it is reasonable to conclude, even in the face of Congress' express deference to state water law in other areas, that the United States intended to reserve the necessary water. Where water is only necessary for a secondary use of the reservation, however, there arises the contrary inference that Congress intended, consistent with its other views, that the United States would acquire water in the same manner as any other public or private appropriator."[62] The *Big Horn* court applied the *New Mexico* rationale to Indian reservations and greatly constrained the ability of the tribe to adjust its water use according to modern day realities.

The Arizona Supreme Court in the *Gila River* adjudication rejected the *Big Horn* approach on two grounds. First, the Arizona Supreme Court said there are enough significant differences between Indian and non-Indian reservations to preclude applying *New Mexico*'s primary-secondary purpose test to Indian water rights cases. The court found chief among these the underlying federal policy of Indian self-sufficiency, which necessitates an interpretation of Indian reserved rights that is broader than that of non-Indian reserved rights.[63] Secondly, the court said, even if the *New Mexico* test applied, the "permanent homeland" purpose would be primary, not secondary.[64]

The debate over what a tribe can do with its *Winters* water gets even more contentious when the issue of off-reservation water marketing is broached. The geography of Indian and non-Indian settlement that emerged from the era of westward expansion is such that today many tribes control large amounts of water upstream from major metropolitan areas.[65] In theory, then, certain tribes could divert water for their own uses and leave little for the already-parched downstream cities. Given this situation, such tribes stand to make a good deal of money by agreeing to not use their water in deference to downstream interests. Marketing water is especially attractive to tribes which possess the rights to reservation water, but lack the infrastructure and resources necessary to exploit it.[66] Under the Nonintercourse Act, tribes are restricted from alienating trust property without specific statutory authorization.[67] There is a limited exception to the Nonintercourse Act, however, which authorizes tribes, with the approval of the Secretary of the Interior, to lease trust land for "public, religious, educational, recreational, residential, or business purposes, including the development or utilization of natural resources in connection with operations under such leases."[68] The use of the term "natural resources" seems to suggest that tribes need only seek the Secretary's approval to market their water.

Even so, difficult questions persist regarding the legality and policy of marketing *Winters* water. First, because most tribes have not had their *Winters* rights quantified, in many situations a reservation's reserved water is already being used for free downstream by those who have consequently built up a substantial reliance interest on this state of affairs. The prospect of suddenly having to pay for water that has for so long been free predictably sparks vehement opposition.[69] Secondly, as discussed throughout this memorandum, the threshold question in water rights cases is often, *what is the purpose of the reservation*? As the Wyoming Supreme Court held, it is very difficult to link the off-reservation marketing of water to the reservation's original purpose, especially if that purpose is an agricultural one.[70] If courts move toward the Arizona Supreme Court's "permanent homeland" approach, water marketing might rest on a much stronger foundation.

TRIBAL REGULATION OF WATER

The Supreme Court has held that Indian tribes, as limited sovereigns, have the right to regulate the conduct of their members,[71] a right which presumably extends to the regulation of members' use of tribal water. States must respect a tribe's right to order its own affairs,[72] and even those states that have assumed criminal and civil jurisdiction over Indian tribes pursuant to Public Law 280 are expressly prohibited from regulating Indian trust water rights.[73]

The real problem with tribal regulation of water arises when tribes attempt to extend their authority to nonmembers. Nonmember water rights arise in two ways: first as mentioned above, an allottee holds rights to a portion of reservation water; second, and even more complicated, homesteaders have rights to reservation water. In the late 1800's and early 1900's some reservations were opened up to the public, and homesteaders moved in to claim portions of reservation land.[74] These homesteaders hold state appropriative water rights,[75] which must be reconciled with the federal reserved water rights of the tribe.

In *Montana v. United States*, the Supreme Court held that a tribe may only regulate the on-reservation activities of *nonmembers* on non-Indian land within the reservation if (1) the nonmembers have entered into consensual relationships (e.g., contracts, leases, etc.) with the tribe; or (2) nonmember conduct on the reservation "threatens or has some direct effect on the political integrity, economic security, or health or welfare of the tribe."[76] Citing their inherent sovereign powers over tribal land and resources, as well as the second *Montana* exception, tribes have enacted water codes purporting to regulate all who use reservation water, sometimes including nonmembers.

The law governing tribal authority to enact water codes regulating nonmembers is not very clear, engendering a great deal of confusion among tribes and private water appropriators.[77] The Department of the Interior (DOI) was sufficiently worried about the potential for conflict inherent in such codes that in 1975 the Secretary imposed a moratorium[78] on all DOI approvals of such water codes submitted by tribes subject to the Indian Reorganization Act (IRA).[79] The moratorium is still in effect, although DOI made one exception in 1985 when it approved the tribal water code included in the water rights compact between the State of Montana and the Assiniboine and Sioux Tribes of the Fort Peck Reservation.[80]

The status of codes enacted by tribes not subject to the IRA is yet to be determined. The available case law, however, suggests that tribal water codes could not be upheld on tribal sovereignty grounds. In *Holly v. Yakima Indian Nation*, a tribe enacted a water code that purported to regulate all use of excess waters on fee lands within the reservation. The court held that nonmember use of excess water on such lands does not implicate the concerns of the second *Montana* exception, and so the exception does not apply.[81] In addition, in *Strate v. A-1 Contractors*, the Supreme Court seemed to limit the second *Montana* exception to those situations where state regulation would impede on "the right of reservation Indians to make their own laws and be ruled by them."[82] It does not appear that tribal water codes regulating nonmembers would satisfy that requirement.

GROUNDWATER

The Supreme Court has never addressed whether a reservation's groundwater is included in its reserved water right. Most states handle groundwater and surface water under separate regulatory and judicial controls,[83] and a determination of rights to groundwater is not required for a McCarran Amendment adjudication to meet its comprehensiveness requirement.[84] The Wyoming Supreme Court, while acknowledging that "the logic that supports a reservation of water to fulfill the purpose of the reservation also supports the reservation of groundwater," refused to extend the *Winters* doctrine to include groundwater because no other court had explicitly done so.[85] Several courts, however, have implicitly recognized a reserved groundwater right.[86] In 1999, the Arizona Supreme Court took the position that the *Winters* doctrine applies to groundwater only when "other waters are inadequate to accomplish the purpose of a reservation."[87] This analysis, the court recognized, essentially dissolves the distinction between surface and groundwater: "The significant question for the reserved rights doctrine is not whether water runs above or below the ground but whether it is necessary to accomplish the purpose of the reservation."[88] This issue is by no means settled.

CONCLUSION

In the century since the Supreme Court promulgated the reserved rights doctrine, the judiciary has often shown itself to be an inadequate body for resolving the myriad of issues that the Court in *Winters* left unresolved, with litigation dragging on endlessly. This is not surprising, given that three governments and tens of thousands of people have significant stakes in the outcomes. The situation in the courts promises to get even more complicated in the wake of the Arizona Supreme Court's *Gila River* ruling.

Many parties have started to realize that issues as complex and important as those outlined in this report are best resolved by settlement, with each party compromising in order to achieve its most important goals. As the drive for a dependable water supply in the Western has grown stronger, so has the desire to quickly settle tribal water claims in order that Western water officials can effectively and accurately plan for the future. In addition, tribes have begun to understand the negotiating power that comes with a reserved water right - power that can be leveraged to address other tribal needs. This transition from courtroom to negotiating table brings with it a larger role for Congress, which must approve each settlement.

Ongoing Adjudications

Presently, there are at least 19 ongoing adjudications involving at least 52 tribes laying claims to water rights on the Gila River, Virgin River, Walker River, Little Colorado River, Milk River, Missouri River, Big Horn River, Tongue River, Rosebud River, Flathead River, Blackfoot River, Bitterroot River, Marias River, Wind River, Klamath River, Snake River, and Yakima River. Initiated in 1977, the Big Horn adjudication, referred to numerous times in this memorandum, reached the Supreme Court once and is currently before the Wyoming Supreme Court for the fifth time.

Pending Settlements

To date, Congress has approved eighteen Indian water rights settlements.[89] Various tribes have negotiated settlement agreements still awaiting Congressional approval, including the Fort Peck Indian Reservation, the Fort Belknap Indian Reservation, and the Aamodt Pueblo Tribe. The Crow Indian Reservation is in the negotiation process and may have a settlement ready to present to Congress within the next few years.

REFERENCES

[1] Benjamin Franklin, Poor Richard's Almanack (1746 ed.).
[2] Studies done by the Western Water Policy Review Advisory Commission found that, from 1972 to 1997, the 17 Western states saw a 32% increase in population, compared to the national average of 19%. In addition, those same studies estimated that the current population of the Western states will increase another 25% by the year 2022. Denise Fort, The Western Water Policy Review Advisory Commission: Another Look at Western Water, 37 Nat. Resources J. 909, 915 (Fall 1997).
[3] Regarding this transition, *see generally* Daniel McCool, Native Waters: Contemporary Indian Water Settlements and the Second Treaty Era (2002).
[4] David H. Getches, Water Law in a Nutshell 6 (3d ed. 1997).
[5] Id.
[6] 207 U.S. 564 (1908).
[7] 207 U.S. at 576.
[8] *Cappaert v. United States*, 426 U.S. 128, 138 (1976). The Colorado Supreme Court has held "appurtenant" water to be that water "on, under or touching the reserved lands." *United States v. City and County of Denver*, 656 P.2d 1, 35 (Colo. 1983).
[9] *Arizona v. California*, 373 U.S. 546, 600 (1963).
[10] *Id.* at 600 (1963).
[11] *Hackford v. Babbit*, 14 F.3d 1457, 1461 (10th Cir. 1994).
[12] The priority date can be even earlier if the water use fits under the category of aboriginal title. In *United States v. Adair*, 723 F.2d 1394, 1414 (9th Cir. 1983), the Ninth Circuit found that the tribe's water rights accompanying its historical right to hunt and fish did not come into being with the reservation, but dated instead to "time immemorial." The court also found that this right is not consumptive in nature, but rather "consists of the right to prevent other appropriators from depleting the stream's water below a protected level in any area where the...right applies." *Id.*, at 1411 (citing *Cappaert v. United States*, 426 U.S. 128, 143 (1976)).
[13] Indian water rights literature is replete with references to the paper water/wet water distinction, which is commonly used to highlight the difference between a right to water versus actually possessing both the water and the means to put it to beneficial use. *See, e.g.*, Daniel McCool, Native Waters: Contemporary Indian Water Settlements and the Second Treaty Era 101 (2002).
[14] *Id*, at 597.

[15] The most glaring example of this conflict is the fact that the Bureau of Indian Affairs and the Bureau of Reclamation are both within the Department of the Interior. In 1970, President Nixon sent a message to Congress pointing out that when such conflicts within Interior arise, "[t]here is considerable evidence that the Indians are the losers." H.R. Doc. No. 363, 91st. Cong., 2d Sess. 10 (1970), *reprinted at* 116 Cong. Rec. 23258, 23261 (1970).
[16] *Nevada v. United States*, 463 U.S. 110, 128 (1983). *See also Cobell v. Babbitt*, 91 F. Supp. 2d 1, 30-31 (D.D.C. 1999) (declining to hold the Secretary of the Interior to common law fiduciary duties, instead looking purely to statute in determining duties owed).
[17] Conference of Western Attorneys General, American Indian Law Deskbook 212 (2d ed. 1998).
[18] Act of July 10, 1952, 66 Stat. 549, 560 (codified at 43 U.S.C. § 666).
[19] 43 U.S.C. § 666(a).
[20] Colorado River Water Conservation District v. United States, 424 U.S. 800, 811 (1976).
[21] *See* Daniel McCool, Native Waters: Contemporary Indian Water Settlements and the Second Treaty Era 75-76 (2002).
[22] Colorado River Water Conservation District v. United States, 424 U.S. 800, 819 (1976).
[23] *See generally* Peter W. Sly, Reserved Water Rights Settlement Manual 177-184 (1988). A Federal Appeals Court has held that a failure to include groundwater in a state general stream adjudication does not invalidate the adjudication on "comprehensiveness" grounds. *United States v. Oregon*, 44 F.3d 758, 768-769 (9th Cir. 1994).
[24] What exactly the power to "administer water rights" entails is not immediately apparent. The most widely followed definition seems to be the one given by a Nevada Federal District Court over thirty years ago: "To administer a decree is to execute it, to ensure its provisions, to resolve conflicts as to its meaning, to construe and interpret its language." *United States v. Hennen*, 300 F.Supp. 256, 263 (D. Nev. 1968).
[25] *See* Conference of Western Attorneys General, American Indian Law Deskbook 220-221 (2d ed. 1998).
[26] In re General Adjudication of All Rights to Use Water in the Big Horn River System, 753 P.2d 76, 114-115 (Wyo. 1988).
[27] Id.
[28] Conference of Western Attorneys General, American Indian Law Deskbook 194 (2d ed. 1998).

[29] See, e.g., Note, Indian Reserved Water Rights: the Winters of Our Discontent, 88 Yale L.J. 1689, 1695 (1979).
[30] United States v. Ahtanum Irrigation District, 236 F.2d 321 (9th Cir. 1956); Conrad Investment Company v. United States, 161 F. 829 (9th Cir. 1908).
[31] See, e.g.,United States v. Walker Irrigation District, 104 F.2d 334, 340 (9th Cir. 1939).
[32] *Arizona v. California*, 373 U.S. 546, 601 (1963).
[33] 373 U.S. at 601.
[34] 373 U.S. at 602.
[35] See, e.g., Jennele Morris O'Hair, *The Federal Reserved Rights Doctrine and Practicably Irrigable Acreage: Past, Present, and Future*, 10 BYU J. Pub. L. 263, 273 (1996). The Supreme Court had an opportunity to clarify its position regarding the PIA standard in *Wyoming v. United States*, but an evenly split Court (made possible by Justice O'Connor's recusal) merely affirmed the Wyoming Supreme Court's judgment without opinion. *Wyoming v. United States*, 492 U.S. 406 (1989).
[36] See Barbara A. Cosens, The Measure of Indian Water Rights: The Arizona Homeland Standard, Gila River Adjudication, 42 Nat. Resources J. 835, 842-844 (Fall 2002).
[37] See, e.g., Fort Mojave Indian Tribe v. United States, 32 Fed. Cl. 29, 35 (1994).
[38] Id.
[39] Id.
[40] *Id*. The *Fort Mojave* court went on to say that "In general, the PIA analysis is grounded upon project development with the overall goal of maximizing the income from the project and not maximizing the water claim."
[41] *See* Peter W. Sly, Reserved Water Rights Settlement Manual 104 (1988).
[42] 492 U.S. 406 (1989).
[43] *See* Andrew C. Mergen and Sylvia F. Liu, *A Misplaced Sensitivity: The Draft Opinions in Wyoming v. United States*, 68 U. Colo. L. Rev. 683 (Summer 1997).
[44] *See, e.g.,* Peter W. Sly, Reserved Water Rights Settlement Manual 104 (1988).
[45] *See, e.g.,* Barbara A. Cosens, *The Measure of Indian Water Rights: The Arizona Homeland Standard, Gila River Adjudication*, 42 Nat. Resources J. 835, 837 (Fall 2002) ("Whereas southern tribes located in alluvial valleys near a large surface water source [e.g. the Colorado River] are entitled under an agricultural purpose quantified by the PIA method to ample water,

tribes in more northern climes or mountainous terrain are left with insufficient rights to meet basic drinking water needs").
[46] In re General Adjudication of All Rights to Use of Water in the Gila River System and Source, 35 P.3d 68, 74 (Ariz. 2002) (quoting Winters, 207 U.S. at 565).
[47] *Id.* at 76.
[48] *Id.* at 79-80.
[49] Act of Feb. 8, 1887, 24 Stat. 388 (codified as amended at 25 U.S.C. §§ 331-334, 339, 341-342, 348-349, 354, 381). For a brief discussion of the history of and policy behind the act, as well as its consequences, *see* F. Cohen, Handbook of Federal Indian Law 127-143 (1982 ed.); *see also* William C. Canby, American Indian Law in a Nutshell 20-23 (3d ed. 1988).
[50] There are several other allotment acts specific to particular tribes, some with longer or shorter trust periods than that of the Dawes Act, but the underlying policy issues from a reserved water rights perspective are the same.
[51] William C. Canby, American Indian Law in a Nutshell 22 (3d ed. 1998).
[52] *See* F. Cohen, Handbook of Federal Indian Law 138 (1982 ed.) ("The majority of Indian lands passed from native ownership under the allotment policy...about 27 million acres, or two-thirds of the total land allotted, passed from Indian allottees by sale between 1887 and 1934. An additional 60 million acres were either ceded outright or sold to non-Indian homesteaders and corporations as 'surplus' lands").
[53] *United States v. Powers*, 305 U.S. 527, 532 (1939). Generally, under the Nonintercourse Act (25 U.S.C. § 177), Indians are forbidden from transferring tribal land without federal government approval, and this prohibition likely applies to the transfer of non-allotted reserved water rights also. *See* Conference of Western Attorneys General, American Indian Law Deskbook 207-209 (2d ed. 1998).
[54] Colville Confederated Tribes v. Walton, 647 F.2d 42, 51 (9th Cir. 1981).
[55] Id.
[56] In re General Adjudication of All Rights to Use of Water in the Gila River System and Source, 35 P.3d 68, 76 (Ariz. 2002).
[57] S. Rifkind, Report of the Special Master - *Arizona v. California* 265 (1962).
[58] In re the General Adjudication of All Rights to Use Water in the Big Horn River System, 835 P.2d 273 (Wyo. 1992).
[59] *Id.* at 278-279.
[60] 438 U.S. 696 (1978).
[61] *Id.* at 718.

[62] Id. at 702.
[63] In re General Adjudication of All Rights to Use of Water in the Gila River System and Source, 35 P.3d 68, 77 (Ariz. 2002).
[64] Id.
[65] For a discussion of the different causes of this state of affairs, see Daniel McCool, Native Waters: Contemporary Indian Water Settlements and the Second Treaty Era 161-163 (2002).
[66] See, e.g., Edmund J. Goodman, Indian Tribal Sovereignty and Water Resources: Watersheds, Ecosystems, and Tribal Co-management, 20 J. Land Resources and Envtl. L. 185, 208 (2000).
[67] 25 U.S.C. § 177. Given the disastrous consequences of the Allotment Act era, discussed earlier, proponents of marketing must overcome some very strong arguments against granting such congressional approval.
[68] 25 U.S.C. § 415.
[69] For this reason, all of the marketing provisions approved so far in water settlement acts specify water delivered from federal projects rather than reserved water.
[70] In re General Adjudication of All Rights to Use Water in the Big Horn River System, 753 P.2d 76, 100 (1988).
[71] *United States v. Wheeler*, 435 U.S. 313, 322 (1978). The Court went on to clarify that the power to punish tribal offenders is an exercise of retained tribal sovereignty. As such, the power "[E]xists only at the sufferance of Congress and is subject to complete defeasance. But, until Congress acts, the tribes retain their sovereign powers. In sum, Indian tribes still possess those aspects of sovereignty not withdrawn by treaty or statute, or by implication as a necessary result of their dependent status." Id. at 323.
[72] Santa Clara Pueblo v. Martinez, 436 U.S. 49, 55 (1978).
[73] 25 U.S.C § 1322.
[74] *See* Peter W. Sly, Reserved Water Rights Settlement Manual 138 (1988).
[75] *United States v. Anderson*, 736 F.2d 1358, 1363-1365 (9th Cir. 1984).
[76] *United States v. Montana*, 450 U.S. 544, 565 (1981).
[77] See generally Thomas W. Clayton, The Policy Choices Tribes Face When Deciding Whether to Enact a Water Code, 17 Am. Indian L. Rev. 523 (1992).
[78] This moratorium is informal and is not codified anywhere, but is commonly known. DOI has told tribes that the Department will not approve their water codes until DOI promulgates regulations pursuant to 25 U.S.C. § 381, which DOI has yet to do. *See Holly v. Totus*, 655 F. Supp. 548, 551-552 (E.D. Wash. 1983). *See also* Conference of Western Attorneys General, American

Indian Law Deskbook 224, n. 250 (2d ed. 1998); Thomas W. Clayton, *The Policy Choices Tribes Face When Deciding Whether to Enact a Water Code*, 17 Am. Indian L. Rev. 523, 548 (1992); Peter W. Sly, Reserved Water Rights Settlement Manual 72 (1988).

[79] 25 U.S.C. § 461 et seq. Congress passed the IRA in an effort to encourage tribal self-government, authorizing tribes to adopt constitutions and by-laws to be ratified by members of the tribe. In order to be effective under the IRA, these constitutions and by-laws must be approved by the Secretary of the Interior.

[80] Memorandum from Ross Swimmer to Secretary of the Interior requesting approval of Fort Peck Water Code, Oct. 7, 1986.

[81] Holly v. Confederated Tribes and Banks of the Yakima Indian Nation, 655 F. Supp. 557, 559 (E.D. Wash. 1985).

[82] *Strate v. A-1 Contractors*, 520 U.S. 438, 459 (1997) (*quoting Williams v. Lee*, 358 U.S. 217, 220 (1959)).

[83] *See* Peter W. Sly, Reserved Water Rights Settlement Manual 181-182 (1988).

[84] *See United States v. Oregon*, 44 F.3d 758, 768-769 (9th Cir. 1994).

[85] *In re General Adjudication of All Rights to Use Water in the Big Horn River System*, 753 P.2d 76, 99 (Wyo. 1988). In addition, a Federal Appeals Court has held that a failure to include groundwater in a state general stream adjudication does not invalidate the adjudication on "comprehensiveness" grounds. *United States v. Oregon*, 44 F.3d 758, 768-769 (9th Cir. 1994).

[86] See Gila River Pima-Maricopa Indian Community v. United States, 695 F.2d 559 (D.C. Cir. 1982); Nevada v. United States, 279 F.2d 699 (9th Cir. 1960); In re Determination of Conflicting Rights, 484 F. Supp. 778 (D. Ariz. 1980); Tweedy v. Texas Co., 286 F.Supp. 383, 385 (D. Mont. 1968).

[87] In re the General Adjudication of All Rights to Use Water in the Gila River System and Source, 989 P.2d 739, 748 (Ariz. 1999).

[88] *Id.*, at 747.

[89] The Gila River Indian Community Water Rights Settlement Act (Title II of P.L. 108-451); The Southern Arizona Water Rights Settlement (Tohono O'odham Nation) (Title III of P.L. 108-451); The Nez Perce/Snake River Water Rights Act (P.L. 108-447, Division J, Title X); The Zuni Indian Tribe Water Rights Settlement Act (P.L. 108-34); The Shivwits Band of the Paiute Tribe of Utah Water Rights Settlement Act (P.L. 106-263); The Chippewa Cree Tribe of the Rocky Boy's Reservation Indian Reserved Water Rights Settlement Act (P.L. 106-163); The Yavapai-Prescott Indian Tribe Water Rights Settlement Act (Title I of P.L. 103-434); The San Carlos

Apache Water Rights Settlement Act (Title XXXVII of P.L. 102-575); The Jicarilla Apache Tribe Indian Water Rights Settlement Act (P.L. 102-441); The Northern Cheyenne Indian Reserved Water Rights Settlement Act (P.L. 102-374); The Fort McDowell Indian Community Water Rights Settlement Act (P.L. 101-628); The Fallon Paiute Shoshone Indian Tribes Water Rights Settlement Act and the Pyramid Lake/Truckee-Carlson Water Rights Settlement Act (Titles I and II, respectively, of P.L. 101-618); The Colorado Ute Indian Water Rights Settlement Act (P.L. 100-585); The San Luis Rey Indian Water Rights Settlement Act (Title I of P.L. 100-675); The Salt River Pima-Maricopa Indian Community Water Rights Settlement Act (P.L. 100-512); The Ak-Chin Indian Water Rights Settlement Act (P.L. 98-530); The Southern Arizona Water Rights Settlement Act (P.L. 97-293).

In: Native Americans: Rights, Laws...
Editor: C. P. Townsend, pp. 71-88

ISBN: 978-1-60456-202-6
© 2008 Nova Science Publishers, Inc.

Chapter 3

NATIVE AMERICAN GRAVES PROTECTION AND REPATRIATION ACT (NAGPRA): LEGAL AND LEGISLATIVE DEVELOPMENTS[*]

Douglas Reid Weimer

ABSTRACT

The Native American Graves Protection and Repatriation Act (NAGPRA) was enacted to serve as a means for museums and federal agencies to return certain Native American cultural items (including human remains) to the lineal descendants, culturally affiliated Indian tribes, or Native Hawaiian organizations. NAGPRA makes provision for both intentionally excavated and inadvertently discovered Native American cultural items on federal and tribal lands. Penalties are provided for noncompliance. A Review Committee was established by NAGPRA to monitor the various processes and to assist in dispute resolution involving repatriation issues.

Certain provisions of NAGPRA were judicially scrutinized in a series of cases concerning the disposition of the remains of an ancient man, believed to be about 9,000 years old and known as the Kennewick Man or the Ancient One, which was discovered on federal land under the jurisdiction of the U.S. Army Corps of Engineers ("COE"). The COE considered the applicability of NAGPRA to the situation, and concluded that NAGPRA was applicable. The COE proposed to return the remains to a coalition of Native American

---

[*] Excerpted from CRS Report RL33031, dated August 10, 2005.

groups. This action was challenged by a group of scientists and others who successfully argued that the provisions of NAGPRA were not applicable. The U.S. Court of Appeals for the Ninth Circuit concluded in *Bonnichsen v. U.S.* that the remains were not identifiable with any current day Native American group, and therefore the provisions of NAGPRA did not apply.

An amendment to NAGPRA has been proposed in section 108 of S. 563, the "Native American Omnibus Act of 2005." If enacted, the amendment would define "Native American" within the context of NAGPRA so as to include a tribe, people, or culture that is or *was* indigenous to any geographic area that is now located within the boundaries of the United States. If enacted, the amendment could have an impact on the ultimate disposition of the remains of the Kennewick Man, as well as the control and custody of any other ancient human remains and related objects which may be discovered.

Interest in NAGPRA is particularly strong during the summer of 2005, as severe weather conditions have caused various rivers in the continental United States–such as the Missouri River–to recede. This has exposed traditional Native American burial grounds which have been subject to increased looting and vandalism.

The Senate Committee on Indian Affairs held oversight hearings on NAGPRA for July 28, 2005. The hearings focused on the proposed amendment contained in S. 563.

INTRODUCTION AND SUMMARY

The Native American Graves Protection and Repatriation Act ("NAGPRA") was enacted by Congress in 1990[1] to provide a means for museums and federal agencies to return such Native American cultural items as human remains, funerary objects, sacred objects, or objects of cultural patrimony to the lineal descendants, culturally affiliated Indian tribes, or Native Hawaiian organizations.[2] NAGPRA also provides for the disposition of unclaimed and culturally unidentifiable Native American cultural items. Provision is made for the inadvertent discovery of Native American cultural items on federal and tribal lands. Penalties are provided for noncompliance with NAGPRA and for the illegal trafficking in cultural goods. The law authorizes federal grants for Indian tribes, Native Hawaiian organizations, and museums to aid with the inventory and return of Native American cultural items. NAGPRA established the Native American Graves Protection and Repatriation Review Committee ("Review Committee"), which is authorized to monitor the various NAGPRA processes and to assist in the resolution of disputes concerning the repatriation of objects or remains. Regulations have been promulgated,[3] and the provisions of the law and the regulations have been implemented. Since NAGPRA's enactment and implementation, many cultural items have been returned to Native American groups and Native Hawaiian organizations.[4]

NAGPRA was perhaps most visible following the discovery of human skeletal remains that are generally believed to be about 9,000 years old and have come to be known as the Kennewick Man or the Ancient One.[5] In 1996 the remains were unexpectedly discovered on federal land administered by the U.S. Army Corps of Engineers ("COE"). The COE considered the application of the provisions of NAGPRA to the Kennewick Man and concluded that NAGPRA was applicable. Pursuant to NAGPRA, the COE proposed to return the remains to a coalition of Native American groups. This action was challenged by a group of scientists and others, who successfully argued that the provisions of NAGPRA were not applicable to the facts in the case. Following extensive litigation, the U.S. Court of Appeals for the Ninth Circuit concluded that the remains were not identifiable with any current day Native American group, and hence the provisions of NAGPRA were not applicable.[6] The remains are currently undergoing scientific testing.

Currently pending legislation, S. 536, the Native American Omnibus Act of 2005,[7] would amend NAGPRA. Section 108 would amend the definition of "Native American," within the context of NAGPRA, so as to include a tribe, people, or a culture, that is or *was* indigenous to the United States (italics added). It would further amend NAGPRA to include the phrase "any geographic area that is now located within the boundaries of" the United States. If enacted, it is not certain what precise impact this amendment may have on the disposition of the Kennewick Man and on the disposition of other ancient human remains which may be discovered in the future. However, if enacted, the amendment may bring such remains into the purview of NAGPRA.[8] The Senate Committee on Indian Affairs held a hearing on S. 536 on July 28, 2005.

The statutory provisions of NAGPRA and the related regulations are outlined below. The factual circumstances concerning the discovery and custody of the Kennewick Man are summarized and the litigation and its conclusions are analyzed. Currently pending legislation, and its possible impact on the application of NAGPRA are considered.

NAGPRA[9]

The search for, excavation, and removal of the contents of Native American graves for profit or curiosity has long been a common practice. It is believed that these activities were at their peak during the late nineteenth century and the early twentieth century. Ultimately, thousands of Native American human remains and funerary objects came to be housed in museums and educational institutions around the United States. For many years, various Indian tribes have tried to have these remains and the funerary objects of their ancestors returned to them. These efforts have often caused heated debates on the rights of the Native American people versus the importance to museums of retaining their collections and the scientific value of the items.[10]

NAGPRA has two main objectives. The first objective concerns prospective excavation or removal of Native American human remains, funerary objects, sacred objects and objects of cultural patrimony from federal or tribal lands. NAGPRA requires that any person who wishes to excavate such items may do so only after receiving a permit issued under the Archeological Resources Protection Act (ARPA).[11] If such remains are found on federal lands and it is known which tribe is related to them, that tribe is afforded the chance to reclaim the remains or objects. If the tribe does not wish to take possession of the remains or objects, the Secretary of the Interior will determine their disposition after consultation with Native American, scientific, and museum groups. NAGPRA also deals with instances concerning the incidental discovery of such items on federal lands by persons engaged in such other activities as construction, logging, or other pursuits. When items are found, the activity must temporarily cease and a reasonable effort is required to be made to protect the discovered items. The federal land manager in charge of the location must be notified in writing and notification must also be given to the appropriate tribe or Native Hawaiian organization, if known or readily ascertainable. NAGPRA provides penalties for selling, or otherwise profiting from, any Native American human remains, associated and unassociated funerary objects, sacred objects, and objects of cultural patrimony currently held or controlled by federal agencies or museums, regardless of their origins..

The second objective of NAGPRA concerns the collections of Native American human remains, associated and unassociated funerary objects, sacred objects, and objects of cultural patrimony held or controlled by federal agencies and museums.[12] NAGPRA required that within five years of its enactment (with discretionary extensions possible), all federal agencies and museums that receive federal funds, which have possession of, or control over, any Native American human remains or associated funerary object, were to compile an inventory of such remains or objects and, with the use of available information, attempt to identify the remains/objects as to geographical and cultural affiliation. Following the completion of the inventory, the appropriate tribe or Native Hawaiian organization was to be contacted. If the tribe or Native Hawaiian organization related to the remains or objects and the tribe or organization wanted the return of the items, the items were to be returned.

A written summary of unassociated funerary objects (those objects known to be funerary objects but not connected to a specific body), sacred objects, and objects of cultural patrimony which are controlled by a federal agency or museum was also to be completed, in this case, within three years of enactment. The summary is to describe the collection, the number of objects in it, and how, when, and from where the collection was received. After the summary, the appropriate Indian tribe or Native Hawaiian organization was to be contacted and the two sides were to meet to discuss the future disposition of the items.

The various museums and federal agencies compiled the requisite inventories and written summaries. Through the utilization of these inventories and the summaries, the museums and the Native American and Native Hawaiian groups have been able to meet and to discuss the appropriate disposition of human remains and various cultural objects. Through the implementation of this consultative process, many objects–including human remains--have been returned to the appropriate Native American and Hawaiian groups.[13] The consultative and repatriation process remains ongoing.

NAGPRA allows for the repatriation of culturally affiliated items in addition to any other agreement for the disposition or caretaking which may be agreed to by the interested parties.

Section-by-Section Summary of NAGPRA[14]

Section 3001[15] provides several key definitions, including the definitions for such terms as "burial site," "cultural affiliation," "Federal agency," "museum," and other related terms. One of the definitions which has come under significant scrutiny is the definition of "Native American":

(9) "Native American" means of, or relating to, a tribe, people, or culture that is indigenous to the United States.[16]

Section 3002 provides for the ownership of various Native American human remains and objects. Native American human remains and objects excavated or discovered on federal or tribal lands after November 16, 1990 are to be repatriated in the following priority sequence: 1) lineal descendants; 2) Indian tribe or Native Hawaiian organization on whose land such objects are discovered; 3) the Indian tribe or Native Hawaiian organization which has the closest cultural affiliation with such remains; and 4) if the cultural affiliation of the objects can not be determined, then the tribe recognized as aboriginally occupying the geographic area may place a claim, or if a different tribe has a stronger cultural relationship to the objects, then that tribe may place a claim.[17] Provision is made for the disposal of unclaimed Native American human remains and objects.[18]

The section provides for the intentional excavation[19] and removal of Native American human remains and objects under certain circumstances. Such activity is permitted only under the provisions of the Archaeological Resources Protection Act (ARPA), after consultation and consent of the related Indian tribe or Native Hawaiian organization, and in accordance with other conditions.

A person inadvertently discovering[20] Native American remains and objects on tribal land or federal land after November 16, 1990 must notify in writing the Department or agency head of the oversight agency in the federal government, and the appropriate tribe or Native Hawaiian organization with respect to tribal lands. If the discovery occurs in the course of an activity such as construction, mining, or logging, the person is required to cease the activity in the area of the discovery, make a reasonable effort to protect the items discovered before resuming such activity, and provide notice. The activity may resume thirty days after certification by the appropriate federal, tribal, or Native Hawaiian official that the notification has been received, the activity may resume thirty days after such certification.[21]

Nothing in this section would prevent the governing body of an Indian tribe or Native Hawaiian organization from expressly relinquishing control over any Native American human remains, or title to or control over any funerary object or sacred object.

Section 3003 sets out requirements for an inventory[22] of human remains and associated funerary objects.[23] Each federal agency and each museum which has possession or control over holdings or collections of Native American human remains and associated funerary objects must compile an inventory of such objects and attempt to identify the geographical and cultural affiliation of each item. Such inventories shall be completed in consultation with tribal government and Native Hawaiian organization officials and religious leaders. Such inventory was required to have been completed not later than November 16, 1995. Native American and Native Hawaiian groups may request additional information from the museum or agency concerning the inventory items. Museums may apply to the Secretary of the Interior ("Secretary") for an extension of time to complete the inventory, if the museum has demonstrated a good faith effort.

If the cultural affiliation of any particular Native American human remains or associated funerary objects[24] is determined, the federal agency or museum concerned, shall notify the affected Indian tribes or Native Hawaiian organization not later than six months after the completion of the inventory. A copy of such notice is to be sent to the Secretary for publication in the Federal Register.

Section 3004 requires that each federal agency or museum that has possession or control over holdings of sacred objects, funerary objects not associated with remains, or objects of cultural patrimony shall provide a written summary[25] of such objects based upon available information held by such agency or museum.[26] The summary is to describe the scope of the collection, the kinds of objects included, geographical locations, acquisition information, and cultural affiliation. Such summary was to have be completed not later than November 16, 1993. Upon request, Indian tribes and Native Hawaiian organizations shall have access to records, catalogues, relevant studies, or other data for determining geographic origin, cultural affiliation, and basic facts surrounding acquisition and accession of Native American objects.

Section 3005 concerns the repatriation of Native American human remains and objects possessed or controlled by Federal agencies and museums.[27] If the cultural affiliation of Native American human remains and associated funerary objects with a particular Native American Indian tribe or Native Hawaiian organization is established, then the federal agency or museum, upon request from a known lineal descendant of the Native American, tribe, or organization, shall return such remains and associated funerary objects. If the cultural affiliation with a particular Indian tribe or Native Hawaiian organization is shown concerning unassociated funerary objects, sacred objects or objects of cultural patrimony, then the federal agency or museum, upon the request of the Indian tribe or Native Hawaiian organization, shall expeditiously return the objects. Where the cultural affiliation of Native American human remains and funerary objects has not been established, such Native American human remains and funerary objects shall be returned when the requesting Indian tribe or Native Hawaiian organization can show cultural affiliation by a preponderance of the evidence based upon geographical, kinship, or other evidence. Similar criteria are to be used for the return of sacred objects and objects of cultural patrimony.[28]

If the lineal descendant, Indian tribe or Native Hawaiian organization requests the return of cultural affiliated Native American cultural items, the federal agency or museum shall return such items, unless such items are indispensable for completion of a specific scientific study, the outcome of which would be of major benefit to the United States. Such items shall be returned by no later than ninety days after the date on which the scientific study is completed.

If there are multiple requests for repatriation of any cultural item, and after complying with the requirements of this chapter, the federal agency or museum cannot determine which person is the most appropriate claimant, the agency or museum may retain the item until the requesting parties agree upon its disposition or the dispute[29] is otherwise resolved pursuant to the statue or by a court.[30]

Section 3006 establishes a Review Committee[31] to monitor and review the implementation of the inventory and identification process and repatriation activities. Criteria are established for the committee. Among the Committee's duties are monitoring the inventory and identification process so as to guarantee a fair, objective consideration and assessment of the available relevant information and evidence; facilitating the resolution of disputes among Indian tribes and others regarding the return of items; and other related activities. The committee is required to make an annual report to Congress regarding the progress and barriers encountered in the implementation of the provisions the legislation. The Committee may be terminated when the Secretary determines, in a report submitted to Congress, that its work has been completed.[32]

Section 3007 provides for penalties.[33] A museum that does not comply with the requirements of NAGPRA may be assessed a civil penalty by the Secretary. Each violation is to be considered a separate offense. The amount of the penalty is to be determined upon the basis of several factors, including the archaeological, historical, or commercial value of the item involved; the damages suffered by the aggrieved party; and the number of violations. If a museum fails to pay the assessment of a civil penalty and has not appealed the penalty, the Attorney General may institute a civil action to collect the penalty. Subpoenas may be issued for the attendance and testimony of witnesses and the production of relevant papers, books, and documents.

Section 3008 provides that the Secretary is authorized to make grants to Indian tribes and Native Hawaiian organizations for the repatriation of Native American cultural items. The Secretary is also authorized to make grants to museums to assist in the inventory and identification processes required by the statute.

Section 3009 concerns savings provisions and provides that nothing in the statute is to limit the authority of any museum or federal agency to return cultural items and to enter into agreements over the disposition of, or control over, cultural items.

Section 3010 states that this statute reflects the unique relationship between the federal government and Indian tribes and Native Hawaiian organizations. The law should not be construed to establish a precedent with respect to any other individual, organization, or foreign government.

Section 3011 provides that the Secretary must promulgate regulations before November 16, 1990.

Section 3012 provides for the authorization of appropriations.

Section 3013 provides that the United States district courts will have jurisdiction over any action alleging a violation of the statute and the courts shall have the authority to issue such orders as may be necessary to enforce the statute.

THE KENNEWICK MAN

Factual and Administrative Background

The Kennewick Man is the name generally given to the remains of a prehistoric man found near Kennewick, Washington, on July 28, 1996.[34] Two teenagers accidently discovered the skull while swimming below the surface in Lake Wallula, a section of the Columbia River pooled behind the McNary Dam. Law enforcement authorities were notified and took charge of the remains.[35] At the time of the discovery of the remains, their age and ethnic origin were uncertain. The land upon which Kennewick Man was found was under the jurisdiction of the U.S. Army Corps of Engineers ("COE").[36]

The Kennewick Man became the focus of debates and extensive litigation about the relationship between Native American cultural and religious rights and science and archaeology. Almost immediately, a controversy developed concerning who was responsible for determining what would be done with the remains. Claims were placed by Indian tribes, local officials, and some members of the scientific community. The COE ultimately took possession of the remains, but its actions to resolve the situation in accordance with NAGPRA were challenged in federal court.

The remains were initially given to forensic anthropologists for study and dating. They concluded that Kennewick Man lived approximately 9,000 years ago. Meanwhile, Indian tribes from the region of the Columbia River opposed the study of the remains on religious grounds and demanded that the remains be turned over to them for immediate burial. Their claim was based on NAGPRA. The COE agreed with the tribal claimants and seized the remains before further testing could be completed. In 1998, the COE and the Secretary of the Interior entered into an agreement whereby the Secretary was given the responsibility to decide whether the remains were "Native American" under NAGPRA, and to determine their appropriate disposition.

Extensive study had indicated that the remains were unlike those of any known present day population, American Indian, or otherwise. Still, based upon the age of the remains and the fact that the remains were found within the United States, the Secretary determined that the Kennewick Man's remains were "Native American" within the meaning of NAGPRA. Later, the Secretary further concluded that the Kennewick remains were culturally affiliated with present day Indian tribes. For this reason, the Secretary awarded Kennewick Man's remains to a coalition of tribal claimants.[37] Pursuant to this decision and in compliance with NAGPRA, the COE published a "Notice of Intent to Repatriate Human Remains" in a local newspaper. Various scientists objected to the repatriation decision and requested that scientists be allowed to study the remains further. The COE did not agree to allow additional study, and the scientists began the litigation.[38]

Judicial Review–*Bonnichsen v. U.S.*

The plaintiffs–a group of scientists and others--challenged the Secretary's decisions in District Court. During the course of this litigation, the scientist-plaintiffs viewed the skeleton as an "irreplaceable source of information about early New World populations that warrants careful scientific inquiry to advance knowledge of distant times."[39] By contrast, the position of the Native American tribes was that the skeleton is "that of an ancestor, who according to the tribes' religious and social traditions, should be buried immediately without further testing."[40]

The Kennewick Man became the focus of debates and extensive litigation about the relationship between Native American cultural and religious rights and science and archaeology. Almost immediately, a controversy developed concerning who was responsible for determining what would be done with the remains. Claims were placed by Indian tribes, local officials, and some members of the scientific community. The COE ultimately took possession of the remains, but its actions to resolve the situation in accordance with NAGPRA were challenged in federal court.

The remains were initially given to forensic anthropologists for study and dating. They concluded that Kennewick Man lived approximately 9,000 years ago. Meanwhile, Indian tribes from the region of the Columbia River opposed the study of the remains on religious grounds and demanded that the remains be turned over to them for immediate burial. Their claim was based on NAGPRA. The COE agreed with the tribal claimants and seized the remains before further testing could be completed. In 1998, the COE and the Secretary of the Interior entered into an agreement whereby the Secretary was given the responsibility to decide whether the remains were "Native American" under NAGPRA, and to determine their appropriate disposition.

Extensive study had indicated that the remains were unlike those of any known present day population, American Indian, or otherwise. Still, based upon the age of the remains and the fact that the remains were found within the United States, the Secretary determined that the Kennewick Man's remains were "Native American" within the meaning of NAGPRA. Later, the Secretary further concluded that the Kennewick remains were culturally affiliated with present day Indian tribes. For this reason, the Secretary awarded Kennewick Man's remains to a coalition of tribal claimants.[37] Pursuant to this decision and in compliance with NAGPRA, the COE published a "Notice of Intent to Repatriate Human Remains" in a local newspaper. Various scientists objected to the repatriation decision and requested that scientists be allowed to study the remains further. The COE did not agree to allow additional study, and the scientists began the litigation.[38]

Judicial Review–*Bonnichsen v. U.S.*

The plaintiffs–a group of scientists and others--challenged the Secretary's decisions in District Court. During the course of this litigation, the scientist-plaintiffs viewed the skeleton as an "irreplaceable source of information about early New World populations that warrants careful scientific inquiry to advance knowledge of distant times."[39] By contrast, the position of the Native American tribes was that the skeleton is "that of an ancestor, who according to the tribes' religious and social traditions, should be buried immediately without further testing."[40]

The district court ruled in plaintiffs' favor and vacated the Secretary's decision on the ground that the Secretary improperly concluded that NAGPRA applied.[41] The district court also held that since NAGPRA did not apply, the plaintiffs should have the opportunity to study Kennewick Man's remains under ARPA. The defendants and the tribal claimants appealed, and the Court of Appeals stayed the district court's order granting the scientists opportunity to study of the remains pending the decision of the Court of Appeals.

In *Bonnichsen v. U.S.*[42] the U.S. Court of Appeals for the Ninth Circuit affirmed the decision of the district court,[43] determining that the scientists had standing to bring this action; that for NAGPRA to apply the human remains must bear some relationship to a presently existing tribe, people or culture to be considered "Native American" within the meaning of NAGPRA; and the evidence did not support the Department of Interior's decision that the remains were Native American within this meaning.[44]

Standing

Following a detailed factual summary of the events leading up to the litigation and a summary of the decisions of the district court, the court turned to the issue of jurisdiction. The tribal claimants argued that the court lacked jurisdiction because the plaintiff's alleged injuries are not redressable by court action and that the plaintiffs lack standing to bring claims alleging violations of NAGPRA because they did not seek to invoke interests within the "zone of interest" protected by NAGPRA. Examining the issue of standing, the court concluded that if NAGPRA does not apply, then the Archaeological Resources Protection Act (ARPA)[45] would apply, and ARPA would give the plaintiffs the opportunity to study the Kennewick Man's remains. The court concluded that the plaintiffs' injury would be redressed by a favorable decision on the NAGPRA issue, and hence the plaintiffs have constitutional standing.[46]

In finding for the plaintiffs, the court rejected the argument of the tribal coalition. The tribal coalition had argued that the plaintiff scientists lacked standing to bring claims alleging violations of NAGPRA. The tribal claimants argued that Congress enacted NAGPRA with the interests of American Indians in mind, and only American Indians or tribes could file suit alleging violations of NAGPRA. The court scrutinized § 3013 of NAGPRA and determined that it did not limit jurisdiction to suits brought by American Indians or Indian tribes.[47]

Concept of "Native American" within the Context of NAGPRA

The court then reviewed the Secretary's decision to transfer the Kennewick Man to the tribal coalition. The court examined NAGPRA and conducted a two-part analysis. The first question is whether the human remains are Native American within the statute's meaning. If the remains are not Native American, then NAGPRA does not apply. If the remains are Native American, then NAGPRA applies, triggering the second question of determining which persons or tribes are most closely affiliated with the remains.[48]

The court focused on the definition of "Native American" at 25 U.S.C. § 3001(9) and noted that the relevant statutory clause is written in the present tense and that the statute unambiguously requires that human remains bear some relationship to a presently existing tribe, people, or culture for them to be considered Native American. The court concluded that Congress enacted NAGPRA to give American Indians control over the remains of their genetic and cultural forebears, not over the remains of people bearing no special and significant genetic or cultural relationship to some presently existing indigenous tribe, people, or culture.[49]

Review of the Secretary's Decision that the Kennewick Man's remains are Native American

The court reviewed the Department of the Interior's records to determine whether there is substantial evidence that supports the agency decision that the Kennewick Man is "Native American" within the context of the NAGPRA definition. After reviewing the record, the court concluded that the record did not contain substantial evidence that the Kennewick Man's remains were Native American within the context of the NAGPRA meaning.

After reviewing all of the records, the court concluded that because the Kennewick Man's remains are so old and that the information about this era is limited, the record did not permit the secretary to reasonably conclude that the Kennewick Man shares special and significant genetic or cultural features with presently existing indigenous tribes, people, or cultures. The court therefore concluded that the Kennewick Man's remains are not Native American remains within the context of NAGPRA, and that NAGPRA does not apply to them.[50]

Consequently, the court ordered that studies of the Kennewick Man's remains by the plaintiff scientists could proceed under ARPA.[51]

Aftermath of the Decision

Following the decision in *Bonnichsen*, studies continue on the remains of the Kennewick Man. Nevertheless, the scientific community is still concerned about the future application of NAGPRA to ancient human remains, as well as about proposed amendments to NAGPRA.

The Umatilla tribe of Native Americans had been a leader of the tribal defendants in the case. The position of the Native Americans is that they wish to have "the remains reburied as required by traditional tribal law...."[52] Although the Native Americans were unhappy with the determinations of the Ninth Circuit, discussed above, they decided not to appeal the case to the U.S. Supreme Court. This decision was based upon the availability of financial resources, the uncertainty of whether the Court would hear the case, and the risk of an unfavorable decision.[53] The position of the tribe, expressed on their website, appears to be that NAGPRA needs to be strengthened so that it fulfills Congress' intent, which was to protect tribal burials and to return sacred items to the tribes.[54]

In fact, Congress has considered legislation to modify the definition of "Native American" within the context of NAGPRA. Legislation was introduced in the 108th Congress to amend NAGPRA. Section 14 of S. 2843,[55] the proposed Native American Technical Corrections Act of 2004, would have amended the definition of the term "Native American" at 25 U.S.C. § 3001(9), so as to add the crucial word "was." The section would have read: "'Native American' means of, or relating to, a tribe, people of culture that is or was indigenous to the United States." If enacted, this change would have expanded the coverage of NAGPRA to potentially include the remains of peoples and cultures which no longer have current descendants, tribal connections, or cultural similarities. The bill was introduced by Senator Campbell on September 23, 2004.[56]

PENDING LEGISLATION – S. 536[57]

S. 536, the Native American Omnibus Act of 2005 was introduced by Senator McCain on March 7, 2005. The purpose of the legislation is to make technical corrections to laws relating to Native American and for other purposes.

Section 108 provides an amendment to the definition of "Native American" within the context of NAGPRA. Two changes are proposed to be made in 23 U.S.C. § 3001(9). If enacted, the amended definition would read:

> (9) "Native American" means of, or relating to, a tribe, people, or culture that is *or was* indigenous to *any geographic area that is now located within the boundaries of* the United States. [amendment language emphasized].

In the accompanying report language,[58] it is stated that this change is intended "to clarify that in the context of repatriations, the term 'Native American' refers to a member of a tribe, a people, or a culture that is or was indigenous to the United States."

Enactment of this amendment may significantly broaden the scope of NAGPRA. As discussed above, the *Bonnichsen* court held that for NAGPRA in its present form to be applicable, there needed to be a connection between the cultural object and a current day people or culture. The amendment would remove such a distinction and would have the possibility of including any indigenous person within the context of NAGPRA, whether or not there is a connection to a current tribal group or culture.

While it cannot be predicted what effect this amendment, if enacted, may have on the ultimate disposition of the remains of the Kennewick Man, it is conceivable that if the amendment to NAGPRA is enacted, there may be further judicial consideration of the applicability of NAGPRA to the Kennewick Man's remains and whether they would fall within the purview of the amended definition of "Native American."

The Senate Indian Affairs Committee held an oversight hearing on NAGPRA on July 28, 2005.[59] The hearing focused on the amendment contained in Section 108 of S. 536. In his testimony before the Committee, an Interior Department official, Paul Hoffman, stated that the Department agrees with the decision in the *Bonnichsen* case.[60] He stated that the Department opposes the amendment to NAGPRA and prefers to let the courts resolve issues of controversy as they did in *Bonnichsen*. This is apparently the first time that the Department has publicly stated that it agrees with the *Bonnichsen* decision and a less expansive application of NAGPRA.[61] His position was supported by the testimony of Paula Barran, the attorney who represented the plaintiff scientists in *Bonnichsen*.

Other witnesses at the hearing included professors and representatives of Native American and Hawaiian groups.[62] Generally speaking, these witnesses supported the amendment to NAGPRA and supported a more expansive and inclusive application of NAGPRA.

REFERENCES

[1] Pub. L. 101-601, Nov. 16, 1990, 104 Stat. 3048. Codified at 25 U.S.C. § 3001 to § 3013.

[2] NAGPRA applies to human remains, funerary objects, sacred objects, or objects of cultural patrimony which are indigenous to Alaska, Hawaii, and the continental United States, but not to territories of the United States. (43 C.F.R. § 10.1(b)(2)).

[3] 43 C.F.R. § 10.1 to § 10.17.

[4] While an exact figure of the number of cultural items repatriated is not readily available, the National Park Service maintains records on its website. The website indicates that the remains of 30,261 individuals, 581,679 associated funerary objects, and 92,298 unassociated funerary objects have been repatriated to the appropriate persons or organizations. See [http://www.cr.nps.gov/nagpra/FAQ/INDEX.HTM].

[5] For the purposes of this report, the ancient human remains will be referred to as the Kennewick Man. This is the designation used by the federal courts

in the related litigation. Native American groups refer to the human remains as the Ancient One.
[6] *Bonnichsen v. U.S.*, 367 F.3d 864 (9th Cir. 2004).
[7] 109th Cong., 1st Sess. (2005).
[8] As discussed below, the circumstances of the Kennewick Man case are unique.
[9] The National Park Service maintains an extensive website concerning NAGPRA, the Review Committee, and related issues. [http://www.cr.nps.gov/nagpra].
[10] H.Rept. No. 101-877 at 10 (1990).
[11] Pub. L. 96-95, §4, Oct. 31, 1979, 93 Stat. 721. Codified at 16 U.S.C. § 470cc.
[12] NAGPRA does not deal with cultural objects in private collections. Repatriation by the Smithsonian Institution is governed by the National Museum of the American Indian Act of 1989 (20 U.S.C. § 80q).
[13] See note 4.
[14] 25 U.S.C. §§ 3001 et seq.
[15] Additional definitions for such terms as "museum," "Federal agency official," and other terms are set out in regulations. (43 C.F.R. § 10.2).
[16] *Id.* § 3001(9).
[17] Federal regulations have been promulgated concerning the custody of human remains, funerary objects, and related objects. (43 C.F.R. § 10.6).
[18] See 43 C.F.R. § 10.8.
[19] Relevant regulations for intentional archaeological excavations are at 43 C.F.R. § 10.3.
[20] Relevant regulations for inadvertent discoveries are at 43 C.F.R. § 10.4.
[21] Regulations have been promulgated concerning consultation between federal agency officials and lineal descendants and other interested parties as part of the intentional excavation or the inadvertent discovery of human remains, funerary objects, sacred objects, or objects of cultural patrimony. (43 C.F.R. § 10.5).
[22] A sample notice of inventory completion is provided in Appendix B, 43 C.F.R. § 10.
[23] Extensive regulations have been promulgated to implement the inventory requirements. (43 C.F.R. § 10.9).
[24] Both associated and unassociated funerary objects are cultural items that are reasonably believed to have been placed with individual human remains either at the time of death, or later as part of the death rite or ceremony of a culture. Under the provisions of NAGPRA, funerary objects are considered

to be "unassociated" if the human remains with which the objects were placed are not in the possession or control of a museum or federal agency. Funerary objects are considered to be "associated" if the human remains with which the objects were placed are in the possession of a museum or federal agency. See 25 U.S.C. § 3001(3).

[25] A sample "summary" is provided in Appendix A, 43 C.F.R. § 10.
[26] Regulations have been promulgated regarding the contents, completion, and other aspects of the summaries of human remains, funerary objects, and other related items in museums and federal collections. (43 C.F.R. § 10.8).
[27] Regulations have been promulgated dealing with repatriation. (43 C.F.R. § 10.10).
[28] Regulations provide for limitations and remedies concerning the return of cultural objects, human remains, and relative objects to native peoples. (43 C.F.R. § 10.15).
[29] Regulations have been promulgated concerning dispute resolution. (43 C.F.R. § 10.17).
[30] Regulations have been promulgated concerning the determination of lineal descent and cultural affiliation. (43 C.F.R. § 10.14).
[31] Regulations have been promulgated concerning the Review Committee. (43 C.F.R. § 10.17).
[32] The Review Committee is operating at the present time. See http://www.cr.nps.gov/ nagpra. Its next meeting is scheduled to be held in November 2005 in Albuquerque, NM.
[33] Regulations have been promulgated at 43 C.F.R. § 10.12.
[34] For the local news of the discovery, see [http://www.kennewick-man.com/kman/news/ story/2888895p-2924726c.html].
[35] See [http://en.wikipedia.org/wiki/Kennewick_man].
[36] See website for the National Park Service Archeology and Ethnology Program: [http://www.cr.nps.gov/aad/kennewick/index.htm].
[37] The factual background is summarized from the court's opinion in *Bonnichsen v. U.S.*, 367 F.3d 864 (9th Cir. 2004).
[38] Id.
[39] 357 F.3d at 869.
[40] Id.
[41] Bonnichsen v. United States, 217 F.Supp. 2d at 1138-39.
[42] 367 F.3d 864 (9th Cir. 2004).
[43] The district court has issued three published opinions in this case. See *Bonnichsen v. United States,* 969 F.Supp. 614 (D.Or. 1997)(denying the defendants' motion to dismiss based on failure to state a claim and ripeness

grounds); *Bonnichsen v. United States,* 969 F.Supp. 628 (D.Or. 1997)(denying defendants' motion for summary judgment and vacating the government's disposition of the Kennewick Man's remains); and *Bonnichsen v. United States,* 217 F.Supp.2d 1116 (D.Or.2002)(again vacating the government's disposition of the Kennewick Man's remains).

[44] In a procedural matter, the original opinion of the Court of Appeals at 357 F.3d 962 (9th Cir.2004) was subsequently amended by a footnote (footnote 20). The amended opinion is at 367 F.3d 864 (9th Cir. 2004).
[45] See note 11.
[46] *Id.* at 872-73.
[47] *Id.* at 873-74.
[48] *Id.* at 875.
[49] *Id.* at 879.
[50] *Id.* at 882.
[51] Id.
[52] See the website for the Confederated Tribes of the Umatilla Indian Reservation at [http://www.umatilla.nsn.ancient.html].
[53] See [http://www.umatilla.nsn.us/kman14.html].
[54] Id.
[55] 108th Cong., 2d Sess. (2004)
[56] The bill was referred to the Committee on Indian Affairs and reported out on November 10, 2004 (S.Rept. 108-406).
[57] 109th Cong., 1st Sess. (2005).
[58] S. Rep. No. 109-67 (2005).
[59] Hearing Before the Senate Committee on Indian Affairs on Native American Graves Protection and Repatriation Act.
[60] *Id.* Testimony of Paul Hoffman, Deputy Secretary for Fish and Wildlife and Parks, U.S. Department of Interior, Washington, DC.
[61] See, "Bush Administration Opposes NAGPRA Amendment," at [http://www.indianz.com/NEWS/2005/009562.asp].
[62] Testimony of Paul Bender, Walter R. Echo-Hawk, Sr., Patricia Lambert, and Van Horn Diamond.

In: Native Americans: Rights, Laws...
Editor: C. P. Townsend, pp. 89-99

ISBN: 978-1-60456-202-6
© 2008 Nova Science Publishers, Inc.

Chapter 4

INDIAN SELF-DETERMINATION AND EDUCATION ASSISTANCE ACT CONTRACTS AND *CHEROKEE NATION OF OKLAHOMA V. LEAVITT*: AGENCY DISCRETION TO FUND CONTRACT SUPPORT COSTS[*]

Nathan Brooks

ABSTRACT

On March 1, 2005, the Supreme Court handed down its decision in *Cherokee Nation of Oklahoma v. Leavitt*. The conflicts in the case (actually two consolidated cases) involved federal agencies' duty to fund contract support costs for contracts with Indian tribes under the Indian Self-Determination and Education Assistance Act (ISDA).

While the case in some ways turned on technical questions of statutory interpretation and appropriations law, it also presented interesting questions regarding the federal government's legal responsibility to honor ISDA contracts and how this responsibility compares to the government's general responsibility to pay contractors. This report includes background on the ISDA, a discussion of the conflicting appeals court decisions, and analysis of the Supreme Court's decision.

---

[*] Excerpted from CRS Report RL32681, dated March 31, 2005.

INTRODUCTION

On March 1, 2005, the Supreme Court issued its decision in two consolidated cases, *Cherokee Nation of Oklahoma v. Leavitt[1]* and *Leavitt v. Cherokee Nation of Oklahoma.[2]* These cases presented interesting questions regarding the Indian Self-Determination and Education Assistance Act (ISDA), federal agencies' responsibility to fund administrative costs for contracts entered into with tribal governments under this act, and how this responsibility compares to the federal government's general responsibility to pay contractors.

BACKGROUND

The history of the relationship between the federal government and America's Indian tribes is characterized not by sequential steps in one certain direction, but rather by periodic policy shifts dramatically altering the direction of the relationship. As a result, the history of this relationship is divided by historians into various periods, such as the allotment era (1887-1934), when the federal government sought to break up Indian reservations into individual allotments of fee simple ownership, and the termination era (1953-1968), when the federal government sought to eliminate the special limited-sovereign legal status that tribes enjoy.

Since the early 1970's, however, the United States has pursued a course of "self-determination" for Indian tribes, under which the federal government encourages the continued existence of the tribal governance structure and allows tribes increasing control over their own destinies. The centerpiece of the self-determination movement is the ISDA,[3] passed by Congress in 1975. The purpose of the act was to transfer planning, conduct, and management responsibilities for certain Indian programs normally carried out by federal agencies (e.g., hospitals and clinics) to the tribes themselves.[4] Consequently, the Department of the Interior and the Department of Health and Human Services (HHS) are authorized to enter into contracts with Indian tribes under which the tribes can conduct and administer these programs.[5] The Secretaries of HHS and Interior – upon request by tribal resolution – must enter into these contracts unless, within sixty days of receiving the tribal resolution, the relevant Secretary finds that certain statutory requirements have not been met.[6]

The Secretaries must devote at least as much funding to these tribally-operated programs as the Secretaries would have devoted to these programs had they been operated by the agencies themselves.[7] This amount of funding is commonly known as the "secretarial amount." In addition, the Secretaries are authorized to issue grants to tribes for a variety of purposes, including improving tribes' abilities to enter into ISDA contracts.[8]

While the ISDA became more successful as an increasing number of tribes took control of government programs operated for their benefit, the original version of the ISDA had a critical shortcoming, in that administrative costs – commonly called contract support costs (CSCs)[9] – were not covered in the secretarial amount. As a result, tribes that assumed programs under ISDA contracts often experienced serious financial shortfalls.[10] Congress moved to remedy this situation in 1988 when it added to the ISDA the following language: "There shall be added to the [secretarial amount] contract support costs which shall consist of an amount for the reasonable costs for activities which must be carried out by a tribal organization as a contractor to ensure compliance with the terms of the contract and prudent management."[11]

Congress also added language in the 1988 legislation conditioning the funding of CSCs on "the availability of appropriations" ("the availability clause")[12] and declaring that "the Secretary is not required to reduce funding for programs, projects, or activities serving a tribe to make funds available to another tribe or tribal organization" ("the reduction clause").[13]

What was perceived as the underfunding of Self-Determination Contracts – particularly with respect to CSCs – continued to be controversial, as agencies failed to fully fund CSCs even after the 1988 Amendments, citing the availability and reduction clauses. In 1999, Congress imposed a one-year moratorium on any new Self-Determination Contracts.[14] In the last few years, Congress, when appropriating funds for ISDA contracts, has placed explicit caps on CSCs, and in doing so has quelled some of this controversy. Questions still remain, however, about the liability – if any – incurred by federal agencies that underfunded CSCs for ISDA contracts before these statutory caps became the norm. To answer this question, one must inquire as to how much discretion the federal agencies possess with regard to these contracts. This issue is at the heart of the conflict in *Cherokee Nation*.

THE ISDA CONTRACTS AND THE CIRCUIT COURT DECISIONS

Both of the consolidated cases that came before the Supreme Court had roots in the same controversy. Since 1983, the Cherokee Nation (the Nation) has carried out many responsibilities transferred to it from IHS under an ISDA compact. The Nation and the HHS Secretary agreed to expand the Nation's responsibilities in 1994 to include the operation of two new IHS clinics, in 1995 to include IHS's Contract Health Care Out-Patient (CHC-OP) physician referral program, and in 1997 to include the In-Patient physician referral program. From 1994-1997, HHS failed to fully pay for the Nation's CSCs.

IHS has established a two-tiered approach for allocating annual appropriated funds to tribes for CSCs; contracts are classified as either "existing" (i.e., those that have already been in operation in previous years) or "new and expanded" (i.e., new contracts or existing contracts that have been modified in the last year).[15] IHS generally allocates funds for existing contracts according to the recommendations of the appropriation committees. Tribes with new and expanded contracts, on the other hand, are placed on a priority list (based on the date of the contract) for their shares of the fund specifically set aside by Congress for these new and expanded contracts ("the ISD Fund"). In practice, this has meant that there is not enough money in the fund to distribute to all the tribes on the list in a given year.[16] IHS did not fully fund the Cherokee Nation's CSCs for either its ongoing contracts or the new and expanded portions of those contracts.

The Cherokee Nation filed a claim for damages against the United States pursuant to the ISDA for failing to fund CSCs, and this claim eventually made its way to the Tenth Circuit, which ruled in favor of the federal government.[17] The Cherokee Nation also filed on its own an administrative claim for breach of contract under the Contracts Disputes Act[18] for failing to fund CSCs. The Federal Circuit Court of Appeals issued a ruling on this claim in favor of the Nation,[19] creating a circuit split.[20]

The Tenth Circuit Decision

At issue for the Tenth Circuit were appropriations for 1996 and 1997. The legislation in those years appropriated to IHS $1.7 and $1.8 billion, respectively, for the administration of the ISDA. While various reports from both the House and Senate Appropriations Committees included recommendations that $160 million should be earmarked for CSCs for existing contracts,[21] neither statute included this restriction. The only ISDA-appropriated money required to be used for a specific purpose, then, according to the statute's language, was $7.5 million required to "remain available" for CSCs.[22]

When IHS allocated funds for CSCs in both years, it did so according to the recommendations contained in the committee reports. Consequently, only $160 million was allocated for ongoing CSCs. The Tribes argued that this was in clear violation of the statutes' explicit language, and that IHS had lump-sum appropriations approaching $2 billion each year from which the Secretary was required by contract to extract monies for CSCs.

The court, however, found in favor of the government, for two primary reasons. First, the court reasoned that the reduction clause necessarily implied a congressional intent that the Secretary have some discretion with regard to those funds, in order to avoid cutting into the budget of other tribal programs. Here, the court touched on what appears to be a fundamental tension between the purpose of the ISDA and the reduction clause: Congress clearly intended to limit the discretion of federal agencies to underfund ISDA contracts, but the reduction clause implies that the federal agencies must have discretion to protect the myriad tribal programs these agencies administer.[23]

The Tenth Circuit also found support for its holding in a later congressional enactment. As mentioned above, Congress in 1998 became concerned and placed a year-long moratorium on new ISDA contracts. In section 314 of that same legislation, Congress inserted the following language:

> Notwithstanding any other provisions of law, amounts appropriated to or earmarked in committee reports for the Bureau of Indian Affairs and the Indian Health Service by...[the 1996 and 1997 appropriations]...for payments to tribes and tribal organizations for [CSCs] associated with self-determination...contracts...with the Bureau of Indian Affairs or the Indian Health Service as funded by such Acts, are the total amounts available for fiscal years 1994 through 1998 for such purposes.[24]

The Tenth Circuit viewed this language as, in essence, enacting the aforementioned earmarking language from the 1996 and 1997 committee reports. In other words, the court ruled, Congress intended to cap the available funds for ongoing contracts at $160 million, and new and expanded CSCs to $7.5 million.[25]

The Federal Circuit Decision

The Federal Circuit began its analysis from a perspective very different from that of the Tenth Circuit. The Federal Circuit used as the touchstone for its analysis certain general principles of appropriations law[26] that, in the court's view, established a presumption that an agency is required to meet its contractual obligations if there is money available to do so. Applied to the facts before it, the Federal Circuit found that HHS had an obligation under its contract with the Cherokee Nation, and this obligation required the Secretary to reprogram unrestricted funds if necessary.[27]

The court rejected the idea that the availability and reduction clauses necessarily vest the Secretary with a certain amount of discretion as to paying CSCs. According to the court, such discretion would be contrary to the purpose of the 1988 ISDA Amendments, which was to remedy the federal agencies' traditional failure to fully fund tribal CSCs.[28] In so finding, the court again diverged significantly from the Tenth Circuit's analytical path.

The Federal Circuit next addressed Section 314 of the 1999 Appropriations Act, which the Tenth Circuit found so compelling. While the Tenth Circuit passed on the question of whether the 1999 language was meant to be retroactive or merely an interpretive guide, the Federal Circuit – foreshadowing the Supreme Court's major concerns – quickly ruled that the 1999 Act could not have retroactive effect because the Tribe's right to payment vested well before that act was passed.[29]

THE SUPREME COURT DECISION

As mentioned above,[30] before the consolidated cases were filed, Congress had in some ways made the debate at issue moot by routinely setting caps on expenditures for CSCs when appropriating funds for ISDA contracts in recent years. Questions still remained, however, about the liability – if any – incurred by federal agencies that underfunded CSCs for ISDA contracts before these statutory caps became the norm.

In addition to the submission of various *amicus curiae* briefs, both parties to the case submitted briefs that focused in large part on the amount of discretion that Congress meant to vest in the agencies with respect to the funding of CSCs in ISDA contracts, and on other issues addressed in the conflicting circuit court opinions. The briefs also revealed the emergence of a question that neither circuit court touched on extensively in its opinion, namely, what are these CSC funding contracts – typical "government procurement contracts" or something different? This question was important, because its answer implicated certain settled principles of government procurement law.

Subsequently, some government contractors expressed concern regarding the possible implications of this case with respect to the government's obligation to pay government contractors generally, and submitted an *amici curiae* brief in favor of the Tribes, expressing the contractors' concern for the possible ramifications of the government's position in this case for non-Indian contractors who regularly do business with the federal government:

> It is critical to understand the practical effect of the government's position. Under the government's view, when a contract to be funded from a general lump-sum appropriation contains a "subject to" clause – as many such government contracts do...the contractor is obligated to perform the contract fully, yet bears the risk that the agency for whatever reasons may exhaust its general appropriation, leaving the contractor not only without payment but also without any legal remedy against the government. The contractor would be forced to rely, in other words, not on Congress' appropriations, but on the uncertain financial management of the agency.[31]

While this issue was not mentioned in either the Tenth or Federal Circuit opinion, during oral arguments, the Supreme Court Justices showed a good deal of interest in the government's obligation to honor contracts generally, and the precedent the Court's decision could set for other government contracts.

The Court's ultimate decision reflected the prominent place this issue had attained as the consolidated cases made their way to the Supreme Court. At the beginning of its opinion, the Court stated its view of the facts before it:

> The Government does not deny that it promised to pay relevant contract support costs. Nor does it deny that it failed to pay ... [The Government] does not deny that, *were these contracts ordinary procurement contracts*, its promises to pay would be legally binding. The Tribes point out that each year Congress appropriated far more than the amounts here at issue (between $1.277 billion and $1.419 billion) for the Indian Health Service 'to carry out' *inter alia*, 'the Indian Self-Determination Act' ... These appropriations Acts contained no relevant statutory restriction[32] [emphasis in original].

The Court further noted that, when possessing adequate unrestricted funds, agencies cannot generally back out of their contractual obligations by reason of insufficient appropriations. From these starting points, the Court framed the issue before it thusly: "If [the government] is...to demonstrate that its promises were not legally binding, it must show something special about the promises here at issue."[33] In other words, in order to avoid application of the general rules of government contracts law, the burden was on the federal agencies to prove that Indian self-determination contracts are not standard government procurement contracts at all, but rather something different. In the Court's view, the agencies did not meet this burden.

Significantly, the Justices rejected the government's argument that ISDA contracts are not really "contracts" at all, but rather agreements by which tribes step into the shoes of the relevant agency. Consequently, the government argued, these tribes – like agencies – are not entitled to receive any amounts promised by Congress. The Court, however, looked at the ISDA's language – as well as its purpose – and gleaned a congressional intent that ISDA contracts be treated like normal government contracts.[34]

The Court's finding that ISDA contracts are no different than general procurement contracts allowed the Justices to easily dispose of the government's aforementioned reduction clause and availability clause arguments.[35] Indeed, the government, in its own brief, had conceded that an agency must honor normal procurement contracts even if the agency has allocated the needed funds for another purpose.[36]

The Court conceded that section 314 of the 1999 Appropriations Act presented a more difficult question, in that the statutory language is easily given to two interpretations. On the one hand, the Court wrote, the language could be read to retroactively bar payment of CSCs for contracts from 1994-1997. On the other hand, the language could be interpreted, in the Court's view, as only prohibiting the use of funds left over from previous years' appropriations to pay CSCs.[37] The Court found, however, that the first interpretation presented possible constitutional difficulties, in that "A statute that retroactively repudiates the government's contractual obligation may violate the Constitution ... And such an interpretation is disfavored."[38] Faced with two interpretations – one of which presented potential constitutional problems and one that did not – the Court followed its own precedent and chose the latter.

CONCLUSION

In sum, the Supreme Court found that ISDA contracts are similar to government procurement contracts and, as such, they bind agencies to honor the payment terms where agencies possess sufficient unrestricted appropriated funds to meet those terms. As IHS here had enough unrestricted money to pay the ISDA contracts in question, the Court ruled in favor of the Tribes.

As mentioned above, Congress has in some ways made the debate at issue in these consolidated cases moot by routinely setting specific caps on expenditures for CSCs when appropriating funds for ISDA contracts in recent years. This case makes clear, however, that Congress must continue to do so if it expects CSCs to be capped. In other words, the decision to cap CSCs must come from Congress, because the federal agencies do not have the discretion to cap payment of CSCs.

REFERENCES

[1] No. 02-1472.
[2] No. 03-853. The citation for the decision is *Cherokee Nation of Oklahoma v. Leavitt*, 453 U.S. __, WL464860 (2005).
[3] P.L. 93-638 (codified, as amended, at 25 U.S.C. §§ 450-450n).
[4] 25 U.S.C. § 450a(b).
[5] *Id.* at § 450f(a)(1). HHS and the Department of the Interior generally carry out their ISDA responsibilities through the Indian Health Service (IHS) and the Bureau of Indian Affairs (BIA), respectively.
[6] If the relevant Secretary finds any of the following to be true of the contract, then the Secretary can refuse to enter into the contract: 1) the services to be rendered will not be satisfactory; 2) adequate protection of trust resources is not assured; 3) the proposed project cannot be properly maintained by the proposed contract; 4) the amount of proposed funding exceeds that allowed under the ISDA; or 5) the proposal includes activities that cannot be carried out by the contractor. *Id.* at § 450f(a)(2).
[7] *Id.* at § 450j-1(a).
[8] *Id.* at § 450h.
[9] These costs generally include financial audits and administrative resources that the Secretaries would not have directly incurred themselves.
[10] *See* S. Rep. No. 100-274, at 7 (1987).
[11] P.L. 100-472, § 205 (codified at 25 U.S.C. § 450j-1(a)(2)).
[12] Parties to ISDA contracts are required to include language mirroring the availability clause in those contracts. 25 U.S.C. § 450l(a).
[13] 25 U.S.C. § 450j-1(b).
[14] *See* S. Bobo Dean and Joseph H. Webster, Symposium: Contract Support Funding and the Federal Policy of Tribal Self-Determination, 36 Tulsa L.J. 349, 351-352 (2000).

[15] This summary of IHS's two-tiered approach is taken from the Tenth Circuit's opinion. *See Cherokee Nation v. Thompson*, 311 F.3d 1054, 1057-1058 (10th Cir. 2002) [hereinafter "Tenth Circuit Decision"]. The IHS has detailed this approach in its IHS Circular No. 96-04.
[16] *See* 10th Circuit Decision, 311 F.3d at 1057-1058.
[17] Tenth Circuit Decision. Joining the Nation in filing this claim was the Shoshone-Paiute Tribe in Nevada, who also argued that IHS failed to fund CSCs in accordance with an ISDA contract.
[18] 41 U.S.C. §§ 601-613.
[19] *Thompson v. Cherokee Nation*, 334 F.3d 1075, 1084-1086 (Fed. Cir. 2003) [hereinafter "Federal Circuit Decision"].
[20] It should be noted that the Ninth Circuit also dealt with this issue, and, like the Tenth Circuit, ruled in favor of the government. *See Shoshone-Bannock Tribes of the Fort Hall Reservation v. Thompson*, 279 F.3d 660 (9th Cir. 2000).
[21] *See, e.g.,* H.R. Rep. No. 104-173, at 97 (1995); S. Rep. No. 104-319, at 90 (1996).
[22] P.L. 104-134; P.L. 104-208.
[23] Tenth Circuit Decision, at 1062.
[24] P.L. 105-277, § 314 (112 Stat. 2681-288).
[25] Tenth Circuit Decision, 311 F.3d at 1064-1065.
[26] Federal Circuit Decision, at 1084-1086.
[27] Id.
[28] *Id.* at 1087-1088.
[29] *Id.* at 1091.
[30] *See, supra,* note 14 and accompanying text.
[31] Brief of *Amici Curiae* for the United States Chamber of Commerce, the National Defense Industrial Association, and the Aerospace Industries Association in Support of the Cherokee Nation and the Shoshone-Paiute Tribes, at 12-13.
[32] *Cherokee Nation of Oklahoma v. Leavitt*, 543 U.S. __ WL464860 (2005) (slip op. at 4).
[33] *Cherokee Nation of Oklahoma v. Leavitt*, 543 U.S. __ WL464860 (2005) (slip op. at 5).
[34] The Court cited, for example, the 426 instances in the ISDA of the word "contract," without any special specifications. *Cherokee Nation of Oklahoma v. Leavitt*, 543 U.S. __ (2005) (slip op. at 6).
[35] *Cherokee Nation of Oklahoma v. Leavitt*, 543 U.S. __ WL464860 (2005) (slip op. at 8-12).

[36] *Cherokee Nation of Oklahoma v. Leavitt*, 543 U.S. __ WL464860 (2005) (slip op. at 9) (citing government's brief).
[37] *Cherokee Nation of Oklahoma v. Leavitt*, 543 U.S. __ WL464860 (2005) (slip op. at 13-14.).
[38] *Cherokee Nation of Oklahoma v. Leavitt*, 543 U.S. __ WL464860 (2005) (slip op. at 14) (citations omitted).

In: Native Americans: Rights, Laws...
Editor: C. P. Townsend, pp. 101-109

ISBN: 978-1-60456-202-6
© 2008 Nova Science Publishers, Inc.

Chapter 5

NATIVE AMERICAN ISSUES IN THE 109TH CONGRESS[*]

Roger Walke

ABSTRACT

Native American issues before Congress are numerous and diverse, covering such areas as federal recognition of tribes, trust land acquisition, gambling regulation, education, jails, economic development, welfare reform, homeland security, tribal jurisdiction, highway construction, taxation, and many more. This report focuses on four Native American issues currently of great salience before Congress: health care, energy, trust fund management reform, and Native Hawaiian recognition.

Thus far, more than 500 bills have been introduced in the 109th Congress that apply, in whole or in part, specifically to Indians,[1] federal Indian programs, or Native Hawaiians. Among the major Native American policy issues of concern to the 109th Congress are:

- Indian health care,
- Indian trust fund management reform,
- Indian gaming lands, and
- Native Hawaiian recognition.

---

[*] Excerpted from CRS Report RS22056, dated September 14, 2006.

Each of these issues is briefly discussed in this chapter.

INDIAN HEALTH CARE

Indian Health Care Improvement Act

Congress has for more than five years been wrestling with the reauthorization of the Indian Health Care Improvement Act (IHCIA; P.L. 94-437, as amended). Federal responsibility for Indian health care is met primarily through the Indian Health Service (IHS) in the Department of Health and Human Services (HHS). While IHS's permanent authorizing legislation, the Snyder Act of 1921, is very broad, the IHCIA authorizes a great many specific IHS programs, ncluding health professional recruitment and retention, mental health services, urban Indian health services, construction and repair of health facilities, various special IHS funds, and IHS reimbursement by Social Security Act health programs (Medicare and Medicaid) and other public and private health insurance programs. Authorizations of appropriations for IHCIA programs expired at the end of FY2001, but Congress continues to appropriate funds for the programs.

Leading Indian health proponents in and out of Congress suggested major changes in IHCIA. A number of significant changes have not been acceptable to HHS or other agencies, however, and ongoing negotiations have produced a succession of IHCIA reauthorization bills through the 106th-109th Congresses. The first IHCIA reauthorization bill introduced in this Congress, S. 1057, was referred to the Senate Indian Affairs Committee and reported on March 16, 2006 (S.Rept. 109-222). A House bill (H.R. 5312), very similar to S. 1057 as reported, was referred to three House committees, and ordered reported by one committee, the Resources Committee, on June 21. A Senate Finance Committee bill, S. 3524, amending the Social Security Act regarding Indian health provisions in Medicaid, Medicare, and SCHIP, was reported by the Committee July 12 (S.Rept. 109-278). For detailed discussion of these bills and Indian health issues, see CRS Report RL33022, *Indian Health Service: Health Care Delivery, Status, Funding, and Legislative Issues.*

INDIAN TRUST FUND MANAGEMENT REFORM

Congress faces a possibly multi-billion-dollar problem stemming from Indian trust funds. The federal government's management of Indian trust funds and lands has led to financial claims against the United States by Indian individuals and tribes. The Indian individual claimants alone suggest they are owed as much as $176 billion. Besides lawsuits, the issue has also led to the controversial reorganization of two agencies, the Bureau of Indian Affairs (BIA) and the Office of Special Trustee for American Indians (OST) within DOI.

The BIA has long managed funds, lands, and related physical assets held in trust for Indian tribes and individuals. Trust lands total about 56 million acres (almost 46 million acres for tribes and 10 million acres for individuals). The funds' asset value recently totaled about $3.3 billion, of which about $2.9 billion was in about 1,400 tribal accounts and $400 million was in more than 260,000 Individual Indian Money (IIM) accounts. The Treasury Department houses the accounts, including making payments to beneficiaries. Historically, the BIA was frequently criticized for its management of trust lands and funds. Investigations and audits in the 1980s and after showed that, among other problems, the BIA could not document the asset values of all trust fund accounts and could not link all trust lands to their owners and accounts. Congress enacted the American Indian Trust Fund Management Reform Act of 1994 to reform the management of Indian trust funds and assets; the act directed the Secretary of the Interior to account for trust fund balances and created the OST to oversee trust management reforms. Two years later, based on the 1994 act and general trust law, IIM account holders filed a class action suit in the federal district court for the District of Columbia against the various U.S. officials, demanding an accounting of their funds and correction of fund mismanagement (*Cobell* v. *Norton*, Civil No. 96-1285, D.D.C.). In addition, at least 25 tribal suits have been filed, covering specific tribes' funds. These events have led to the current reorganization of the BIA and OST and to congressional consideration of the settlement of IIM and tribal claims arising from trust fund and lands mismanagement.

Claims and Settlement[2]

In the first of two stages of the *Cobell* case, the district court in 1999 found that DOI and Treasury had breached their trust duties regarding (1) the document retention and data gathering necessary for an accounting and (2) the business systems and staffing to fix trust management. The court ordered DOI and

Treasury to bring trust management up to current trust standards. The final stage of the lawsuit will determine the amount of money that ought to be in the IIM plaintiffs' accounts. In an intervening stage, the district court decided what historical accounting method should be used to determine the amount owed the plaintiffs. DOI in 2003 proposed reconciling all trust account transactions above a certain value but only a sampling of transactions below that value, back to 1938, while the plaintiffs had proposed using production and mapping databases and DOI data to estimate the total amount due. DOI estimated its method would show IIM losses in the tens of millions, while the plaintiffs' methods have shown estimated losses (including interest) of well over $100 billion.

The district court has twice issued orders (September 2003 and February 2005) requiring the DOI to perform a historical accounting of all IIM trust account transactions and assets since 1887, without using statistical sampling. After the second order, DOI estimated that compliance would cost $12-13 billion. Both times the U.S. Court of Appeals for the D.C. Circuit overturned the district court's order. To date the district court has not issued another order on historical accounting. The DOI continues to carry out its historical accounting plan.

Congress has acted on the *Cobell* suit chiefly through oversight hearings and through provisions in Interior appropriation acts and reports. Both the House Appropriations Committee and the conference committee, in their reports on the FY2006 Interior appropriations act (P.L. 109-54), stated that they rejected the position that Congress intended in the 1994 Act to require an historical accounting on the scale of that ordered by the district court, but no bills have been introduced in this Congress to amend the 1994 Act to delineate the extent of the historical accounting obligation.

Congress has long been concerned that the costs of the Cobell lawsuit may jeopardize DOI trust reform implementation, reduce spending on other Indian programs, and be difficult to fund. Current costs include the expenses of the ongoing litigation. Possible future costs include $12-$13 billion for the court-ordered historical accounting, a Cobell settlement that might cost as much as the court-ordered historical accounting, the $27.5 billion that the Cobell plaintiffs have proposed as a settlement amount (in their statement of principles for settlement legislation), or the more than $100 billion that Cobell plaintiffs estimate their IIM accounts are owed. Among the funding sources for these large costs are discretionary appropriations and the Treasury Department's "Judgment Fund," although some senior appropriators consider the Fund insufficient for a $12-$13 billion dollar settlement, much less a larger one. Among other options, Congress may await further court actions, delay a court-ordered accounting, delineate DOI's historical accounting obligations, or direct a settlement. Thus far two settlement bills, S. 1439 and H.R. 4322, have been introduced in the 109th Congress. Both bills would establish an IIM accounting-claim settlement fund (whose size was left blank in the introduced bills) from which payments would be distributed to IIM claimants (under a formula to be determined by the Treasury Secretary), establish a commission to review and recommend changes in Indian trust asset management, allow increased payments for fractionated individual Indian trust interests, create a tribal trust management demonstration project, combine BIA and OST under a new Under Secretary for Indian Affairs, and require an annual independent audit of all Indian trust funds (for detailed discussion, see CRS Report RS22343, *Indian Trust Fund Litigation: Legislation to Resolve Accounting Claims in Cobell v. Norton*). The Senate Indian Affairs Committee held hearings on S. 1439 in July 2005 (S.Hrg. 109-194) and March 28, 2006 (S.Hrg. 109-483), and, with the House Resources Committee, on both bills on March 1, 2006 (S.Hrg. 109-441). H.R. 4322 awaits further committee action. Senate Indian Affairs Committee mark-up of an amended S. 1439, with a settlement amount of $8 billion, was scheduled for August 2 but withdrawn at the Administration's request, pending more negotiations over including IIM land mismanagement claims as well as IIM accounting and funds mismanagement claims under the $8-billion settlement.[3]

Reorganization

The DOI, BIA, and OST have undertaken, or proposed, a number of administrative and organizational changes to implement trust management reform since the 1994 Act. One of the more important changes was the 1996 transfer from BIA to OST of the office that manages the trust funds; management of trust lands and other physical assets stayed with BIA. In April 2003 the DOI undertook a new, and ongoing, reorganization that splits the BIA trust management operations off from other BIA services at the regional and agency levels, and creates OST field operations (by placing fiduciary trust officers and administrators at BIA regional and agency offices) to oversee trust management and provide information to Indian trust beneficiaries. Tribal leaders and the *Cobell* plaintiffs vigorously oppose the current reorganization, claiming it included insufficient consultation with tribes, insufficiently defined new OST duties, and should have followed, not preceded, creation of new trust management procedures. The DOI responded that it had consulted with tribes for a year beforehand and that it had faced a court-ordered deadline. Attempts to halt the reorganization in recent Congresses have been defeated, and bills in previous Congresses proposing various changes in DOI and BIA trust management, such as abolishing OST, assigning trust line authority to a new office, or establishing a commission to recommend improvements in federal Indian trust laws and policies, have not been reported from committee. S. 1439 and H.R. 4322, however, as noted above, propose to reorganize DOI management of Indian trust assets, and S. 1439 may be marked up pending the negotiations mentioned above.

INDIAN GAMING LANDS

The Indian Gaming Regulatory Act (IGRA; P.L. 100-497) was enacted to provide a regulatory structure for gambling on Indian reservations and certain other lands, with the intent that tribes would use gaming revenues for tribal economic development and governmental programs. IGRA prohibits gaming on any trust lands acquired after its enactment in 1988, but allows eight exceptions to this prohibition, including ones for tribes without reservations in 1988, newly recognized tribes, restored tribes, and land-claim settlements, and in circumstances where the Interior Secretary and the state governor agree that the acquisition would benefit the tribe and not harm the local community. Critics assert that the exceptions allow "reservation shopping," where tribes seek trust lands for gaming "off-reservation" (i.e., distant from tribes' existing reservations or current or historic locations), and also undermine the on-reservation economic development intended by Congress and encourage land claims and investor-funded tribal petitions for federal acknowledgment.

Two of the bills introduced to curb the exceptions, S. 2078 and H.R. 4893, have been reported. Both bills delete the exception requiring secretarial and gubernatorial agreement, but allow applications filed before a certain 2006 date (March 7 for H.R. 4893, April 15 for S. 2078) to go forward, although H.R. 4893 adds a geographic limitation to lands with a "nexus" to the tribe. Both bills retain exceptions for tribes without reservations in 1988, newly recognized tribes, and restored tribes (but with limitations for the latter two exceptions, including a tribal land "nexus," Interior Secretary approval, and, for H.R. 4893, a tribal-local mitigation agreement). The land claim exception is repealed by H.R. 4893 but retained by S. 2078 although with geographic and legal limitations. H.R. 4893 adds a new exception for tribes landless on the date of its enactment, but applies the same limits as for newly recognized tribes. Opponents object that the bills add new and unfair burdens on newly recognized, restored, and landless tribes, that the exceptions for secretarial/gubernatorial agreements and land claims have been used only rarely since 1988, and especially that H.R. 4893's requirement for mitigation agreements is an unprecedented subjection of tribal sovereignty to local governments. S. 2078 awaits Senate floor action. H.R. 4893 was considered by the House September 13 and failed to pass. (For more information, see CRS Report RS21499, *Indian Gaming Regulatory Act: Gaming on Newly Acquired Lands*.)

NATIVE HAWAIIAN RECOGNITION

Native Hawaiians, the indigenous people of Hawaii, are not currently considered Indians under federal Indian law and have no political entity that, like Indian tribes, is recognized by the federal government. Congress has however authorized a number of federal programs to benefit Native Hawaiians. Supporters of recognition are concerned that the absence of a recognized Native Hawaiian political entity endangers federal and state Native Hawaiian programs, exposing them to current legal challenges that claim the programs are race-based. At present, Indian tribes are usually recognized either by Congress or through the DOI's administrative process; Native Hawaiians, however, are excluded from the DOI process, which means congressional action is needed for a Native Hawaiian political entity to be recognized. Three bills in the 109th Congress, S. 147, H.R. 309, and S. 3064, would establish a process by which a Native Hawaiian political entity would be organized and federally recognized. The bills leave for later negotiations (and legislation) questions concerning the political entity's governmental powers and lands, and exclude the Native Hawaiian political entity from BIA programs and from coverage under the Indian Gaming Regulatory Act. Some of the arguments for and against the bills are summarized here.

Proponents argue that Congress has power to recognize a Native Hawaiian political entity because Congress's constitutional authority over "commerce with ... the Indian tribes" extends to all indigenous native peoples in the United States. They also argue that Congress has recognized a "special political and legal relationship with the Native Hawaiian people" (S. 147, §2(21)) identical with that with Indian tribes. They point to the numerous Native Hawaiian programs that Congress has established, especially the Hawaiian homelands program, which was established in 1921 when Hawaii was a territory but is now under Hawaii state control (with certain continuing congressional duties), under which certain public lands are reserved for lease only to Native Hawaiians. Proponents argue that Native Hawaiians have not given up their claims to sovereignty but rather had sovereignty forcibly withdrawn in the 1893 overthrow of the Kingdom of Hawaii, an action led by Americans living in Hawaii and with the active support of certain

U.S. officials and armed forces there. (The new Republic of Hawaii agreed to U.S. annexation in 1898.) They further state that Native Hawaiians, like Indian tribes, have maintained a single distinct community, with cultural and political institutions.

Opponents dispute these points. They argue that Congress's authority extends only to Indian tribes, not to all indigenous peoples, and that hence Congress does not have constitutional authority to recognize a Native Hawaiian political entity. A September 2005 Justice Department statement echoed this concern over constitutionality. Opponents also argue that the United States does not have a special responsibility to Native Hawaiians as it has for Indian tribes. Opponents also contend that recognition of a Native Hawaiian political entity would be based on race alone, arguing that unlike Indian tribes the Native Hawaiian entity would not need to meet criteria of geography, community, and continuous political autonomy. They argue further that Native Hawaiian recognition would set a precedent for political recognition of other, race-based, non-Indian groups. For instance, the U.S. Civil Rights Commission on May 5, 2006, issued a briefing report opposing passage of S. 147 as reported, citing racial discrimination concerns. In addition, some opponents dispute the claims regarding Native Hawaiian sovereignty, arguing among other things that Native Hawaiians' sovereignty ended well before 1893 because the kingdom gave political rights to non-Native Hawaiians, or that sovereignty resided in the monarch, not the Native Hawaiian people, and ended with the 1893 overthrow.

Bills similar to S. 147 and H.R. 309 received extensive consideration in the previous three Congresses. S. 147 was reported by the Senate Indian Affairs Committee on May 16, 2005 (S.Rept. 109-68). S. 3064, an amended version of S. 147 introduced May 25, 2006, is based on discussions among congressional offices, the Administration, and the state of Hawaii. The Senate on June 8, 2006, failed to invoke cloture on a motion to proceed to consider S. 147, effectively ending Senate consideration of S. 147 and S. 3064. H.R. 309 was referred to the House Resources Committee and has not been reported. Separately, the House Judiciary Committee's Subcommittee on the Constitution held a hearing on July 19, 2005, on constitutional issues raised by H.R. 309 (Serial No. 109-37).[4]

REFERENCES

[1] In this report, the term "Indian" means American Indians and Alaska Natives (the latter term includes the American Indians, Eskimos (Inuit and

Yupik), and Aleuts of Alaska); the term "Native American" means Indians and Native Hawaiians.

[2] For a legal analysis and history of the *Cobell* case, see CRS Report RS21738, *The Indian Trust Fund Litigation: An Overview of* Cobell v. Norton. Case documents and further information are available at the plaintiffs' and the Justice Department's websites, at [http://www.indiantrust.com] and [http://www.usdoj.gov/civil/cases/cobell/index.htm], respectively.

[3] "McCain Puts Twist in Cobell Settlement Legislation," Indianz.com, Aug. 3, 2006, available at [http://www.indianz.com/News/2006/015273.asp].

[4] For further analyses of legal and other issues, see CRS Report RL33101, S. 147/H.R. 309: Process for Federal Recognition of a Native Hawaiian Governmental Entity.

In: Native Americans: Rights, Laws... ISBN: 978-1-60456-202-6
Editor: C. P. Townsend, pp. 111-119 © 2008 Nova Science Publishers, Inc.

Chapter 6

CHILD CUSTODY PROCEEDINGS UNDER THE INDIAN CHILD WELFARE ACT: AN OVERVIEW[*]

Kamilah M. Holder

ABSTRACT

In 1978, Congress enacted the Indian Child Welfare Act (ICWA) in response to legislative findings of harm caused to Indian children, their families, and tribes by the high separation rate of Indian children from their homes and cultural environments. Congress addressed this situation by granting Indian tribes and Indian parents an enhanced role in determining when to remove Indian children from their homes and cultural environments. Specifically, the ICWA enumerates provisions for tribal jurisdiction and tribal intervention in state court proceedings concerning the custody, adoption, foster care placement, and termination of parental rights of Indian children.

No bills amending the ICWA were introduced in the 109th Congress. Still, the debate over provisions of the ICWA remains an issue of concern. This CRS report provides an overview of some of the goals and provisions of the Indian Child Welfare Act.

---

[*] Excerpted from CRS Report RS22554, December 14, 2006.

BACKGROUND

Congress enacted the Indian Child Welfare Act (ICWA)[1] in 1978 to address the high rate of separation of Indian children from their homes and cultural environments.[2] Prior to 1978, as many as 25 to 35 percent of the Indian children in some states were removed from their homes and placed in non-Indian homes.[3] This practice of removal fragmented families and threatened the continued survival of Native American tribes. Respect for the self-determination of tribes required, in the view of Congress, that tribes be given a greater say in decisions affecting Indian children.[4] In evaluating the perceived biases of state agencies, the House report accompanying the legislation cited the apparent inability of social workers to accord proper recognition to factors in Indian environments that tended to mitigate the severe economic deprivations found on many reservations, deprivations that often served as a basis for state agency neglect findings.[5] The legislative history also indicated that Indian parents often lacked adequate legal representation in child custody proceedings and were frequently coerced into voluntary waivers of their parental rights.[6] As a result, addressing the situation was thought to require both procedural and substantive components to promote a policy of stability and security for Indian tribes and families while also ensuring that the foster and adoptive homes of Indian children reflected the unique values of Indian culture.[7]

COVERAGE

The ICWA applies to Indian children involved in certain child custody proceedings. For purposes of the ICWA, an Indian child is an unmarried individual under age 18 who is either a member of a federally recognized Indian tribe or the biological child of a member of a tribe and eligible for membership in a tribe.[8] Membership eligibility is evaluated by tribes and the requirements vary widely by tribe.[9] Under the ICWA, Indian custodians include any Indian person with legal custody of an Indian child under tribal laws, customs, state laws or "to whom temporary physical care, custody, and control has been transferred by the parent of such child."[10] The ICWA applies in the following child custody proceedings:

- a foster care placement;[11]
- any action "resulting in the termination of the parent-child relationship";[12]
- a pre-adoptive placement that consists of "the temporary placement of an Indian child in a foster home or institution after the termination of parental rights but prior to or in lieu of adoptive placement;"[13] and
- an adoptive placement, which refers to the final placement of an Indian child for adoption including any action that results in a final decree of adoption.[14]

However, "child custody proceeding" does not include an award of custody in a divorce proceeding; nor does it include a placement based upon an action by the child that would be a crime if committed by an adult.[15]

JURISDICTION

Among the most important elements of the ICWA are its jurisdictional provisions. In enacting the ICWA, Congress recognized that Indian tribes have distinct societal interests in the lives of Indian children that can be distinguished from that of the parents. In preserving these interests, the ICWA both enhances the jurisdictional reach of tribal courts and provides a right of intervention in state court proceedings that involve Indian children.[16] In part, the act delineates areas of exclusive tribal jurisdiction and those of concurrent state and tribal jurisdiction.

Exclusive Tribal Jurisdiction

Under the ICWA, an Indian tribe generally has exclusive jurisdiction over an Indian child who resides or is domiciled within the tribe's land.[17] Indian tribes also have exclusive jurisdiction over Indian children who are wards of a tribal court that has previously exercised jurisdiction over their cases.[18] There are two exceptions to the grant of exclusive tribal jurisdiction. Tribal courts do not have jurisdiction where jurisdiction is "otherwise vested in the State by existing Federal law."[19] The other exception is the emergency removal of a child who resides or "is domiciled on the reservation, but temporarily located off the reservation, from his parent or Indian guardian in order to prevent imminent physical harm."[20] Under the ICWA, federal, state and tribal courts must all afford full faith and credit to the orders and judgments of a tribal court that has exercised jurisdiction in an Indian child custody proceeding.[21]

Concurrent Jurisdiction

In child custody proceedings involving Indian children not residing or domiciled on the tribe's land, the ICWA confers concurrent jurisdiction on tribal and state courts.[22] The ICWA expresses a preference for tribal jurisdiction in child custody proceedings involving Indian children. As such, state court proceedings that address foster care placement or termination of parental rights and involve Indian children residing or domiciled off the reservation may be transferred to tribal courts. This transfer shall take place upon the petition of either parent, the Indian custodian or the child's tribe unless one of the child's parents objects, the tribal court declines jurisdiction or good cause to deny transfer exists.[23] The first two exceptions present very little room for judicial analysis; however, the "good cause" exception is a broader area of judicial interpretation. Guidelines, issued by the Department of the Interior, state that a party opposing transfer to a tribal court bears the burden of demonstrating good cause to deny transfer.[24] The Guidelines also provide examples of what constitutes good cause.[25]

Judicial Decisions

The only U.S. Supreme Court case to address the ICWA dealt with the statutory construction of the act's domicile provision and how it was to be interpreted. In *Mississippi Band of Choctaw Indians v. Holyfield*, the Supreme Court determined that for purposes of the ICWA a child's domicile at birth is that of his or her parents at the time of birth.[26] In reaching this decision, the Court reasoned that the purpose of the statute indicated congressional intent to establish uniformity in the application of the ICWA, instead of allowing varied state court definitions of a key term to dictate ICWA application. Thus, the Court held that an Indian tribe had jurisdiction over twin baby girls whose parents took care to have the children born off the reservation in order to put the children up for adoption under state law.

State courts have developed different approaches to addressing general questions of ICWA applicability and such other concerns as the grounds for invoking the "good cause" exception to transfer. For example, some state court judicial decisions scrutinize the level of contact between an Indian child and the Indian tribe or reservation, while other courts engage in a "best interests of the child" analysis in assessing possible reasons for transfer.[27] Other courts have dealt with the issue of applying the judicially crafted "existing Indian family exception" with varying results.[28]

Procedural Protections in State Courts

In expanding the ability of tribes to strengthen and preserve Indian families, the ICWA not only enhances tribal jurisdiction but also provides comprehensive procedural protections for Indian tribes, parents and custodians throughout state court proceedings. For example, where a state court knows or has reason to know at the outset of an involuntary custody proceeding that the child at issue is an Indian child, the ICWA requires that the party seeking termination of parental rights or foster care placement notify the child's parent or Indian custodian and tribe.[29] Notice must be given at least ten days before the advancement of the state proceedings.[30] Tribes must be notified of their unconditional right to intervene in the state court proceeding and their right to examine all relevant documents as well as their ability to obtain a delay of the proceedings.[31] These provisions are all aimed at ensuring that parents, custodians and tribes are aware of their rights under the ICWA and are given adequate time to exercise these rights.

Additional provisions, applicable in both voluntary and involuntary cases, are also intended to ensure that Indian parents, custodians and tribes are not misled or coerced into losing their rights to rear Indian children. As such, cases that proceed in state courts are subject to a number of procedural protections, whether the proceeding is voluntary or involuntary. Voluntary proceedings consist of tribal member parents choosing termination of parental rights and adoption or foster care placement of their child. Involuntary proceedings involve state attempts to terminate parental rights or place Indian children in foster care. Tribes may intervene in both involuntary and voluntary proceedings. Also, an Indian child's tribe, parent, Indian custodian or an "Indian child who is the subject of an action for foster care placement or termination of parental rights under state law" may seek to invalidate the action upon a showing that the action violated provisions of the ICWA.[32]

Voluntary Proceedings

For any voluntary placement to be valid, the consent of the Indian parent must be in writing and executed before a judge of a court of appropriate jurisdiction. The judge must certify that the consequences of the action to be undertaken are explained to the parent in a language that the parent understands. The consent to the termination of parental rights cannot be executed until after the child is 10 days old.[33] Indian parents can revoke their consent at any time during their child's foster care placement or before a decree of termination or adoption has been entered.[34] Upon revoking consent, the parent would be entitled to the immediate return of the child. However, in cases of adoption where an order accepting the voluntary termination of parental rights has been entered, then the parent may not revoke consent.

Involuntary Proceedings

First, the party seeking foster care placement or the termination of parental rights must provide notice of the proceedings to the parent or Indian custodian and the child's tribe.[35] The ICWA gives indigent parents or Indian custodians the right to court-appointed counsel in any involuntary removal, placement or termination proceeding.[36] In involuntary proceedings, the parties also have the right to examine all reports or other documents filed with the court on which any decision may be based.[37] Furthermore, a state court cannot order an involuntary foster care placement unless it determines that the parent's or Indian custodian's continued custody of the child is likely to result in serious emotional or physical damage to the child.[38] The determination must also meet the clear and convincing standard and be based on evidence that includes testimony from at least one qualified expert witness.[39] In order to terminate parental rights or initiate foster care placement in regard to an Indian child, a state court must ensure that active efforts have been taken to provide remedial services and rehabilitative programs to Indian parents and custodians in order to prevent the breakup of the Indian family.[40]

Adoptive Placements

The ICWA also addresses adoption. The ICWA establishes an order of preference for adoptive placement of an Indian child under state law, "in the absence of good cause to the contrary," that looks to placing a child with extended family members, other members of the tribe or Indian families.[41] Also, the ICWA establishes a placement preference plan to be followed in foster care and preadoptive placements.[42] Tribes may establish a different order of preference by resolution, to be followed in the aforementioned placements.[43]

Proposed Legislation

Although there have been attempts to amend the ICWA in earlier Congresses,[44] no legislative proposals to amend the Indian Child Welfare Act were introduced in the 109th Congress.

REFERENCES

[1] P.L. 95-608, 92 Stat. 3069 (1978); codified at 25 U.S.C. §§ 1901 -1963.
[2] 25 U.S.C. § 1901(4). This embodies a congressional finding that an alarmingly high number of Indian children were being removed from their homes by nontribal public and private agencies and often placed in non-Indian institutions or homes.
[3] H.Rept. 95-1386, 95th Cong., 2d Sess. 9 (1978).
[4] Id.
[5] Id.
[6] Id.
[7] 25 U.S.C. § 1902.
[8] 25 U.S.C. § 1903(4). Under 25 U.S.C. § 1903(8), " 'Indian tribe' means any Indian tribe, band, nation or other organized group or community of Indians recognized as eligible for the services provided to Indians by the Secretary of the Interior because of their status as Indians, including any Alaska Native village as defined in section 1602(c) of Title 43."
[9] Cohen's Handbook of Federal Indian Law § 3.03[2] (Nell Jessup Newton et al. eds., 2005 ed.) [hereinafter Cohen's Handbook].
[10] 25 U.S.C. § 1903(6).
[11] 25 U.S.C. § 1903(1)(i). "Foster care placement" encompasses placements in which the parent or Indian custodian cannot have the child returned upon demand but the parent's rights have not been terminated.
[12] 25 U.S.C. § 1903(1)(ii).
[13] 25 U.S.C. § 1903(1)(iii).
[14] 25 U.S.C. § 1903(1)(iv).
[15] 25 U.S.C. § 1903(1).

[16] 25 U.S.C. § 1903(12) defines tribal court as "a court with jurisdiction over child custody proceedings and which is either a Court of Indian Offenses, a court established and operated under the code or custom of an Indian tribe, or any other administrative body of a tribe which is vested with authority over child custody proceedings."
[17] 25 U.S.C. § 1911(a).
[18] Id.
[19] 25 U.S.C. § 1911(a). This exception most often applies in states that have assumed civil jurisdiction over Indian reservations under laws such as Public Law 280 (25 U.S.C. §1321-25). (Public Law 280 is the popular name of P.L. 83-280, as amended, a law conferring jurisdiction over activities in most of the Indian country in specified states to state courts.) However, in these circumstances, 25 U.S.C. §1918 authorizes tribes to retake jurisdiction over child custody proceedings upon approval by the Secretary of the Interior.
[20] 25 U.S.C. § 1922.
[21] 25 U.S.C. § 1911(d).
[22] 25 U.S.C. § 1911(b).
[23] 25 U.S.C. § 1911(b).
[24] Guidelines for State Courts; Indian Child Custody Proceedings; 44 Fed. Reg. 67,584 (Nov. 29, 1979).
[25] *See* id. at 67,591 (Guideline C.3(b)(i) and (iii)).
[26] 490 U.S. 30 (1989).
[27] Cohen's Handbook § 11.03.
[28] *Compare, e.g., In re Adoption of Baby Boy L,* 643 P.2d 168 (Kan. 1982) (court did not apply provisions of ICWA over the objections of a child's Indian father and his tribe after finding that the child had no ties to his Indian father or the tribe and was not part of an existing Indian family) *and In re Baby Boy C,* 805 N.Y.S.2d 313, 27 A.D.3d 34 (N.Y. 2005) (court declined to adopt the "existing Indian family exception" on the grounds that it was inconsistent with the provisions of the ICWA).
[29] 25 U.S.C. § 1912(a).
[30] Id.
[31] Id.
[32] 25 U.S.C. § 1914.
[33] 25 U.S.C. § 1913(a).
[34] 25 U.S.C. § 1913(b).
[35] 25 U.S.C. § 1912(a).
[36] 25 U.S.C. § 1912(b).

[37] 25 U.S.C. § 1912(c).
[38] 25 U.S.C. § 1912(e).
[39] 25 U.S.C. § 1912(f).
[40] 25 U.S.C. § 1912(d).
[41] 25 U.S.C. § 1915(a).
[42] 25 U.S.C. § 1915(b).
[43] 25 U.S.C. § 1915(c).
[44] Marcie Yablon, *The Indian Child Welfare Act Amendments of 2003*, 38 Fam. L.Q. 689 (2004-2005) (discussing proposals to, *e.g*, address judicial decisions that put certain children beyond the reach of the ICWA because they were not part of an "existing Indian family").

In: Native Americans: Rights, Laws... ISBN: 978-1-60456-202-6
Editor: C. P. Townsend, pp. 121-129 © 2008 Nova Science Publishers, Inc.

Chapter 7

INDIAN GAMING REGULATORY ACT: GAMING ON NEWLY ACQUIRED LANDS[*]

M. Maureen Murphy

ABSTRACT

The Indian Gaming Regulatory Act (IGRA) (P.L. 100-497) generally prohibits gaming on lands acquired for Indians in trust by the Secretary of the Interior (SOI) after the date of enactment of IGRA, October 17, 1988. The exceptions, however, may be significant because they raise the possibility of Indian gaming proposals for locations presently unconnected with an Indian tribe. Among the exceptions are land: (1) contiguous to or within reservation boundaries; (2) acquired after the SOI determines acquisition to be in the best interest of the tribe and not detrimental to the local community and the governor of the state concurs; (3) acquired for tribes that had no reservation on the date of enactment of IGRA; (4) acquired as part of a land claim settlement; (5) acquired as part of an initial reservation for a newly recognized tribe; and (6) acquired as part of the restoration of lands for a tribe restored to federal recognition. On October 5, 2006, the Bureau of Indian Affairs (BIA) of the Department of the Interior (DOI) issued a proposed regulation to specify the standards that must be satisfied by tribes seeking to conduct gaming on lands acquired after October 17, 1988. The proposal includes limiting definitions of some of the statutory terms and considerable specificity in the documentation required for such applications. Legislative proposals include H.R. 1654 and H.R. 2562, which contain

---
[*] Excerpted from CRS Report RS21499, dated June 8, 2007.

provisions to tighten the standards for tribes to secure exceptions to IGRA's prohibition on gaming on lands acquired after 1988, and several bills dealing with recognition of particular tribes or transfers of specific pieces of property (S. 310/ H.R. 505, S. 375/H.R. 679, H.R. 28, H.R. 65, H.R. 106, H.R. 673, and H.R. 1294), which include provisions that preclude gaming.

REQUIREMENTS FOR GAMING ON "INDIAN LANDS"

The Indian Gaming Regulatory Act (IGRA)[1] provides a framework for gaming on "Indian lands,"[2] according to which, Indian tribes may conduct gaming that need not conform to state law. The three classes of gaming authorized by IGRA progress from class I social gaming, through class II bingo and non-banking card games, to class III casino gaming.[3] One of the requirements for class II and class III gaming is that the gaming be "located in a State that permits such gaming for any purpose by any person, organization or entity."[4] The federal courts have interpreted this to permit tribes to conduct types of gaming permitted in the state without state limits or conditions. For example, tribes in states that permit "Las Vegas" nights for charitable purposes may seek a tribal-state compact for class III casino gaming.[5] On the other hand, the fact that state law permits some form of lottery or authorizes a state lottery is not, in itself, sufficient to permit a tribal-state compact permitting all forms of casino gaming.[6]

GEOGRAPHIC EXTENT OF IGRA GAMING

A key concept of IGRA is its territorial component. Gaming under IGRA may only take place on "Indian lands." That term has two meanings. (1) "all lands within the limits of any Indian reservation"; and (2) "any lands title to which is either held in trust by the United States for the benefit of any Indian tribe or individual or held by any Indian tribe or individual subject to restriction by the United States against alienation and over which an Indian tribe exercises governmental power."[7] Under the first alternative, gaming under IGRA may take place on any land within an Indian reservation, whether or not the tribe or a tribal member owns the land and whether or not the land is held in trust. Determining the applicable boundaries of a reservation is a matter of congressional intent and may entail a detailed analysis of the language of statutes ceding tribal reservation land, and the circumstances surrounding their enactment as well the subsequent jurisdictional history of the land in question.[8]

The second alternative has two prongs: (a) the land must be in trust or restricted[9] status, and (b) the tribe must exercise governmental authority over it. Determining trust or restricted status involves Department of the Interior (DOI) records. Determining whether a tribe exercises governmental authority may be a simple factual matter involving whether the tribe has a governmental organization that performs traditional governmental functions such as imposing taxes.[10] On the other hand, it could be a matter requiring judicial construction of federal statutes.[11]

How Land Is Taken into Trust

Congress has the power to determine whether to take tribal land into trust.[12] There are many statutes that require DOI to take land into trust for a tribe or an individual Indian.[13] An array of statutes grant the Secretary of the Interior (SOI) the discretion to acquire land in trust for individual Indian tribes; principal among them is the Wheeler-Howard, or Indian Reorganization Act of 1934.[14] Procedures for land acquisition are specified in 25 C.F.R., Part 151. By this process Indian owners of fee land, i.e., land owned outright and unencumbered by liens that impair marketability, may apply to have their fee title conveyed to SOI to be held in trust for their benefit. Among the effects of this process is the removal of the land from state and local tax rolls and the inability of the Indian owners to sell the land or have it taken from them by legal process to collect on a debt or for foreclosure of a mortgage.

"Indian Lands" Acquired after Enactment of IGRA

Lands acquired in trust after IGRA's enactment are generally not eligible for gaming if they are outside of and not contiguous to the boundaries of a tribe's reservation. There are exceptions to this policy, however, that allow gaming on certain "after acquired" or "newly acquired" lands. One exception permits gaming on lands newly taken into trust with the consent of the governor of the state in which the land is located after SOI: (1) consults with state and local officials, including officials of other tribes; (2) determines "that a gaming establishment on the newly acquired lands would be in the best interest of the Indian tribe and its members"; and (3) determines that gaming "would not be detrimental to the surrounding community."[15]

OTHER EXCEPTIONS FOR GAMING ON LAND ACQUIRED AFTER OCTOBER 11, 1988

Other exceptions permit gaming on after-acquired land and do not require gubernatorial consent, consultation with local officials, or SOI determination as to tribal best interest and effect upon local community. They relate to any of five circumstances:

1. Any tribe without a reservation on October 17, 1988, is allowed to have gaming on newly acquired lands in Oklahoma that are either within the boundaries of the tribe's former reservation or contiguous to other land held in trust or restricted status by SOI for the tribe.[16]
2. If a tribe that had no reservation on October 17, 1988, and is "presently" located in a state other than Oklahoma, it may have gaming on newly acquired lands in that state that are "within the Indian tribe's last recognized reservation within the State."[17]
3. A tribe may have gaming on lands taken into trust as a land claim settlement.[18]
4. A tribe may have gaming on lands taken into trust as the initial reservation of a tribe newly recognized under the Bureau of Indian Affairs' process for recognizing groups as Indian tribes[19];
5. A tribe may have gaming on lands representing "the restoration of lands for an Indian tribe that is restored to federal recognition."[20]

PROPOSED REGULATION FOR GAMING ON NEWLY ACQUIRED TRUST LANDS

On October 5, 2006, the Bureau of Indian Affairs (BIA) issued a proposed regulation setting standards that DOI will use in determining whether class II or class III gaming may take place on after-acquired lands.[21] With respect to the two-part determination, the proposal includes : (1) a requirement that the application for a gaming determination on land not yet in trust must be filed at the same time as the application to have the land taken into trust; (2) a definition of "surrounding community" that covers local governments and tribes within a 25-mile radius; (3) detailed requirements as to projections which must accompany the application respecting benefits to the tribe and local community, potential detrimental effects, and proposals to mitigate any detrimental effects.

The proposed regulation includes a level of specificity that may prove controversial. Indian gaming interests may criticize elements of the proposed regulation as too restrictive; opponents of gaming may seek further limiting interpretations of various statutory language. On the other hand, some may find that the proposed regulation involves a degree of specificity that will further transparency, thereby improving the deliberative process as well as the ability of potential challengers to assess the pros and cons of appealing SOI decisions on land acquisition for gaming. For example, applicants must provide information on: (1) distance of the land from tribal "core governmental functions"; (2) consulting agreements; (3) financial and loan agreements; (4) proposed programs for compulsive gamblers; (5) impact costs to the local community and means of mitigation; (6) projected benefits to the relationship between the tribe and the local community; and (7) "anticipated impacts on the social structure, infrastructure, services, housing, community character, and land use patterns of the surrounding community." [22] Upon determining that a trust acquisition is in the best interest of the tribe and not detrimental to the local community, SOI must notify the state's governor, who must act within one year, with a possible one-time 180-day extension, or SOI will inform the applicant tribe that the application is no longer under consideration.

Unlike earlier proposed regulations, issued for public comment but never finalized,[23] the current proposal is not limited to the two-part SOI determination. It also covers: (1) newly acquired contiguous lands, defining "contiguous" to include parcels separated by non-navigable waters or a public road or right-of-way; (2) initial reservations for newly acknowledged tribes, requiring the land to be "within an area where the tribe has significant historical and cultural connections," and located within 50 miles of the tribal headquarters or within a 50-mile radius of the residences of a majority of the tribe's members; (3) "restored lands" for a tribe restored to federal recognition, requiring that if "restoration legislation does not provide geographic parameters ... the tribe [must have] ... a modern connection and a significant historical connection to the land and ... a temporal connection between the date of the acquisition of the land and the date of the Tribe's restoration"; and (4) land acquisitions under land claim settlements, by requiring that the land must have been acquired in trust as part of the settlement of a land claim filed in federal court or included in DOI's list of potential pre-1966 claims and involving a relinquishment of the tribe's legal claim to land or a return to the tribe of "tribal lands identical to the lands claimed by the tribe." [24] The proposal also specifies how a tribe may establish its connection to land, both in modern times and historically.

LEGISLATION

To date, in the 110th Congress, two bills, H.R. 1654 and H.R. 2562, have been introduced addressing the process by which gaming may be authorized on newly acquired lands. H.R. 1654 would apply the two-part SOI determination, but not the gubernatorial concurrence, to the exceptions for land claim settlements, initial reservations for newly recognized tribes, and restored lands for newly restored tribes. H.R. 2562 would require the state legislature as well as the governor to concur in the SOI two-part determination and eliminate the exceptions for land claim settlements, initial reservations for newly recognized tribes, and restored lands for newly restored tribes.

There are other bills, moreover, which would prohibit gaming in connection with providing federal recognition to a certain tribe or entity or transferring land to a particular tribe. Among them are:

- S. 310 and H.R. 505. These bills provide a process for federal recognition of a Native Hawaiian governing entity and preclude gaming by that entity.
- S. 375 and H.R. 679. These bills would remove a particular limitation presently applicable to a parcel of real property in Marion County, Oregon, deeded by the United States to the Confederated Tribes of Siletz Indians of Oregon and the Confederated Tribes of the Grand Ronde Community of Oregon, and preclude gaming on the land.
- H.R. 28. This would transfer certain land in Riverside County, California, and San Diego County, California, from the Bureau of Land Management to be held in trust for the Pechanga Band of Luiseno Mission Indians, and restrict the use of the lands to "protection, preservation, and maintenance of the archaeological, cultural, and wildlife resources thereon."
- H.R. 65. This would provide federal recognition for the Lumbee Tribe and preclude tribal gaming.
- H.R. 106. This would provide federal recognition for the Rappahannock Tribe and preclude gaming on lands taken into trust for the tribe.

- H.R. 673. This would direct the SOI to take lands in Yuma County, Arizona, into trust as part of the reservation of the Cocopah Indian Tribe and prohibit IGRA gaming on those lands.
- H.R. 1294. This would provide federal recognition for six Virginia Indian tribes and preclude tribal gaming.

REFERENCES

[1] P.L. 100-497, 102 *Stat.* 2467, 25 U.S.C. §§ 2701 - 2721; 18 U.S.C. §§ 1166 - 1168.
[2] 25 U.S.C. § 2703(4).
[3] 25 U.S.C. §§ 2703((6) - (8), and 2710.
[4] 25 U.S.C. §§ 2710(b)(1)(A), and 2710(d)(1)(B).
[5] *Mashantucket Pequot Tribe v. State of Connecticut*, 737 F. Supp. 169 (D. Conn. 1990), *aff'd*, 913 F.2d 1024 (2nd Cir.1990), *cert. denied*, 499 U.S. 975 (1991). Compacts may prescribe, with exacting detail, the specifics of each game permitted. See, e.g., the compact between New York State and the Seneca Nation, Appendix A, listing 26 permitted games and the specifications for each. Available at [http://www.sni.org/gaming.pdf], when visited April 10, 2003.
[6] Rumsey Indian Rancheria of Wintun Indians v. Wilson, 64 F. 3d 1250 (9th Cir. 1994), opinion amended on denial of rehearing, 99 F. 3d. 321 (9th Cir. 1996), cert. denied, 521 U.S. 1118 (1997); State ex rel. Clark v. Johnson, 120 N.M. 562; 904 P. 2d 11 (1995).
[7] 25 U.S.C. § 2703(4).
[8] See, e.g., *South Dakota v. Yankton Sioux Tribe*, 522 U.S. 329 (1998); *Solem v. Bartlett*, 465 U.S. 463 (1984).
[9] "Restricted fee land" is defined to mean "land the title to which is held by an individual Indian or tribe and which can only be alienated or encumbered by the owner with the approval of the SOI because of limitations in the conveyance instrument pursuant to federal law." 25 C.F.R. § 151.2 If restricted land is involved, it may only be considered "Indian lands," for IGRA purposes if the tribe "exercises governmental power" over it. *Kansas v. United States*, 249 F. 3d 1213 (10th Cir. 2001), held that a tribe could not accept governmental authority by consent from owners of restricted land whom the tribe had accepted into membership.
[10] See, e.g., *Indian Country U.S.A., Inc. v. Oklahoma*, 829 F. 3d 967 (10th Cir. 1987), involving a tribe that exercised taxing authority.

[11] See, e.g., *Rhode Island v. Narragansett Tribe of Indians,* 816 F. Supp 796 (D. R.I. 1993), *aff'd, modified,* 19 F. 3d 685 (1st Cir. 1994), *cert. denied* 513 U.S. 919 (1994). This case held that, despite the fact that a federal statute conveyed civil and criminal jurisdiction over a tribe's reservation to a state, the criterion of exercising governmental power was satisfied by various factors including federal recognition of a government-to-government relationship, judicial confirmation of sovereign immunity, and a federal agency's treatment of the tribe as a state for purposes of administering an environmental law.
[12] U.S. Const. art. I, § 8, cl. 3 (Indian Commerce Clause), and *id.,* art. IV, § 3, cl. 2 (Property Clause).
[13] See, e.g., § 707 of the Omnibus Indian Advancement Act, P.L. 106-658, 114 Stat. 2868, 2915, 25 U.S.C. § 1042e, mandating that the SOI take any land in Oklahoma that the Shawnee Tribe transfers.
[14] Act of June 18, 1934,ch. 57, 48 *Stat.* 985, 25 U.S.C. § 465. This statute specifies that such land is to be exempt from state and local taxation.
[15] 25 U.S.C. § 2719(b)(1).
[16] 25 U.S.C. § 2719(a)(2)(A)(i) and 2719(a)(2)(A)(ii).
[17] 25 U.S.C. § 2719(a)(A)((2)(B). There are other specific exceptions for certain lands involved in a federal court action involving the St. Croix Chippewa Indians of Wisconsin and the Miccosukee Tribe of Indians of Florida. 25 U.S.C. § 2719(b)(2).
[18] Under this provision SOI took into trust a convention center in Niagara Falls, N.Y, now being used for casino gaming by the Seneca Nation, on the basis of legislation settling disputes over the renewal of 99-year leases in Salamanca, N.Y., 25 U.S.C. §§ 1174, et seq.
[19] See CRS Report RS21109, *The Bureau of Indian Affairs' Process for Recognizing Groups as Indian Tribes,* by M. Maureen Murphy. In an opinion on "Trust Acquisition for the Huron Potawatomi, Inc.," the DOI Solicitor General's office stated that "the first time a reservation is proclaimed ..., it constitutes the 'initial reservation' under 25 U.S.C. § 2719(b)(1)(B), and the ... [tribe] may avoid the ban on gaming on 'newly acquired land' for any lands taken into trust as part of the initial reservation — those placed in trust before or at the time of the initial proclamation. Land acquired after the initial proclamation of the reservation will not fall within the exception." Memorandum to the Regional Director, Midwest Regional Office, Bureau of Indian Affairs 2 (December 13, 2000). [http://www.nigc.gov/LinkClick.aspx?link=NIGC   +Uploads%2

findianlands%2f33_nottawaseppihuronpotawatomibnd.pdf and tabid=120 and mid=957].
[20] 25 U.S.C. § 2719(b)(iii).
[21] 71 *Fed. Reg.* 58769. The comment period was extended to February 1, 2007, 71 Fed. Reg. 70335 (December 4, 2006); 71 Fed. Reg. 70335 (January 17, 2007), and corrections issued. 71 Fed. Reg. 70335.
[22] Proposed 25 C.F.R. § 292.17 and 292,18, 71 *Fed. Reg.* 58769, 58774-58775..
[23] 65 *Fed. Reg.* 55471 (September 14, 2000). An earlier proposal, 57 *Fed. Reg.* 51487 (July 15, 1991) was never issued in final form.
[24] Proposed 25 C.F.R. §§ 292.2, 292. 5, 292.6, 292.7, and 292.11. 71 *Fed. Reg.*58769, 58774-58775.

In: Native Americans: Rights, Laws... ISBN: 978-1-60456-202-6
Editor: C. P. Townsend, pp. 131-138 © 2008 Nova Science Publishers, Inc.

Chapter 8

STATE REGULATION OF TRIBAL LANDS IN NEW YORK: CITY OF SHERRILL V. ONEIDA INDIAN NATION OF NEW YORK[*]

Nathan Brooks

ABSTRACT

On March 29, 2005, the Supreme Court issued its decision in *City of Sherrill v. Oneida Indian Nation of New York*, a case with serious implications for the State of New York's ability to regulate tribal lands within New York. A federal appeals court had ruled that the Oneida Indian Nation could, by purchasing former reservation lands illegally alienated from the tribe, reestablish the reservation status of those lands and thereby shield them from state taxation. The Supreme Court reversed this decision, holding that the passage of time between the illegal conveyance and the claim in this case barred the Oneidas' attempt to reassert sovereignty over the land in question.

---

[*] Excerpted from CRS Report RS22107, dated April 6, 2005.

BACKGROUND

The relationship between state and tribal power on tribally-owned lands has always been an uneasy one, particularly when the question of a state's ability to levy taxes on such lands arises. The Constitution vests the federal government with exclusive power with respect to Indian tribes,[1] and the Supreme Court has held that, "as a corollary of this authority, and in recognition of the sovereignty retained by Indian tribes even after formation of the United States, Indian tribes and individuals generally are exempt from state taxation within their own territory."[2] Consequently, while Congress can allow states to tax Indians within reservation land, this congressional intent must be expressed in "unmistakably clear" terms in order to be recognized by the courts.[3]

The Facts of *Sherrill*

Some dispute exists as to when the Oneida Reservation in New York was formally established. However, the federal government acknowledged the existence of such a reservation in 1794 when Congress ratified the Treaty of Canandaigua,[4] which included a promise by the federal government that "the said reservation shall remain theirs, until they choose to sell the same to the people of the United States *who have the right to purchase*"[5] (emphasis added). Twenty years later, New York began pressuring the tribes residing within the state's borders – including the Oneidas – to remove to the western territories, and many did so. The Oneidas sold much of their Reservation lands to New York State and to other non-tribal-members. Significantly, these purchasers bought the land without the consent of the federal government, despite the Indian Nonintercourse Act's requirement that such consent be obtained before purchasing tribal land.[6]

This practice of removal – in essence, paying tribes to move west – picked up steam in other states, and by the 1830's it was the policy of the federal government to encourage eastern tribes to exchange their land for lands set aside in the West.[7] In order to facilitate the removal of the Indians still remaining in New York at the time, the United States entered into the Treaty of Buffalo Creek with the various New York tribes. In 1838, Congress ratified the treaty,[8] in which the approximately 5,000 remaining Oneidas agreed to "remove to...[Kansas], as soon as they can make satisfactory arrangements with the Government of the State of New York for the purchase of their lands in Oneida."[9] The remaining Oneidas never removed to Kansas, and the last 150 years have been dotted with frequent litigation over the validity of the Oneida sales and the rights of the Oneidas vis-avis the original reservation land.[10]

In 1985, the Supreme Court ruled that the Oneidas could recover damages against several counties for violating the Oneidas' aboriginal rights to land unlawfully conveyed to and occupied by those counties.[11] The Court specifically left open the question, however, of whether "equitable considerations should limit the relief available to the present day Oneida Indians."[12] The Court's ruling spurred more litigation concerning how much money the Oneidas and other similarly-situated New York tribes are owed. Currently, several of these tribes are engaged in settlement negotiations with the State of New York. Reportedly, the settlement agreements would allow these tribes to build casinos in the Catskill mountains.[13]

The particular dispute in *Sherrill* began in the 1990's, when the Oneidas started buying back parcels of former Reservation land – several in particular located in Sherrill. On two of these properties ("the Sherrill properties"), the Oneidas operated a gas station, convenience store, and textile facility. The Oneidas refused to pay property taxes or to collect sales taxes related to the Sherrill properties, arguing that the properties are within their reservation, and so are free from state and municipal taxation.[14] Following the Oneidas' refusal to pay taxes, Sherrill offered some of the properties at tax sales and instituted eviction proceedings.

THE LOWER COURT RULINGS AND POSSIBLE RAMIFICATIONS

The tribal and municipal parties brought their dispute to court, the essential question being: did the Oneidas' land regain its reservation status when it was repurchased by the Oneidas, in light of the fact that the federal government never approved the original sale that alienated the land from the Oneidas? The District Court answered this question in the affirmative,[15] and the municipal parties appealed to the Second Circuit Court of Appeals. The major question, according to the Second Circuit, was whether the Oneida Reservation had been explicitly disestablished by Congress. The municipal parties pointed to the aforementioned Treaty of Buffalo Creek as evincing Congress's intent to disestablish the Oneida Reservation. In examining this argument, the court used two well-settled principles for interpreting Indian treaties: 1) Indian treaties are to be construed liberally in favor of the Indians, and ambiguous terms are to be interpreted to their benefit; and 2) congressional intent to abrogate Indian treaty rights can only be found with the help of explicit statutory language to that effect.[16]

With these principles in mind, the Second Circuit examined the Buffalo Creek Treaty. The court found that while certain articles of the treaty implicitly disestablished various reservations with language evincing an intent that the tribes in question would remove, the Oneidas conditioned their removal on future arrangements between the Oneidas and the Governor of New York. Because these agreements were never made, the court concluded, the Reservation was never disestablished.[17] As reservation land, then, it could not be alienated without express approval of the federal government, of which there was none in this case. The court held that when Indian land has, as here, been alienated in ways inconsistent with federal law, the tribe retains aboriginal Indian title to the land, and if the tribe at some point buys the land back, the land reverts to its former reservation status, largely free from state taxation.[18]

Potential Ramifications of the Second Circuit's Holding: *Cayuga Indian Nation*

While the Second Circuit's holding was limited to taxation, the rationale behind that holding – that Indian tribes can reacquire former tribal lands and thereby reestablish the reservation status of such lands – had potentially broad consequences for state regulation of tribal activities in other areas, most notably Indian gaming. This was evidenced by the federal district court ruling in *Cayuga Indian Nation of New York v. Village of Union Springs*.[19]

In *Cayuga Indian Nation*, the tribe made an argument nearly identical to that put forward by the Oneidas. Like the Oneidas, much of the Cayugas' treaty land had been sold to the State of New York – without the federal government's permission – in the late eighteenth and early nineteenth centuries. In 2003, the Cayugas reacquired some of that land, and went ahead with plans to build a bingo hall on the property. The village of Union Springs attempted to halt construction pursuant to the city's zoning and construction ordinances, while the tribe argued that the land is part of the tribe's reservation and, therefore, the Indian Gaming Regulatory Act (IGRA)[20] – not municipal regulation – governs gambling facilities on the land. Relying largely on the Second Circuit's rationale with respect to the Oneidas, the district court held that the Cayugas' title to the land in question could only have been legally divested by Congress. Because that never happened, the reservation never ceased to exist, and the tribes reestablished the reservation status of the land when they repurchased it.[21] The court agreed with the tribe that the bingo hall project was "governed by IGRA, which preempts state and local attempts to regulate gaming on Indian lands."[22]

THE SUPREME COURT'S HOLDING

The Supreme Court approached the facts before it in *Sherrill* from an entirely different angle from the lower courts or either of the parties. Indeed, as the Court wrote, "We resolve this case on considerations not discretely identified in the parties' briefs."[23] As mentioned above, in 1985 the Supreme Court found that, while the Oneidas were entitled to damages for the illegal conveyance and occupation of lands to which they held aboriginal title, the Court explicitly left open the question of whether "equitable considerations should limit the relief available to the present day Oneida Indians."[24] The Court viewed the Oneidas' claims in *Sherrill* as a chance to answer this question. In other words, this case was not about the status of the land, as the Second Circuit thought, but rather the *type of remedy* due to the Oneidas for the wrongful occupation of that land. The Court, then, framed the Oneidas' claim thusly: "[The Oneida Nation] seeks declaratory and injunctive relief recognizing its present and future sovereign immunity from local taxation on parcels of land the Tribe purchased in the open market, properties that had been subject to state and local taxation for generations."[25]

Re-casting the Oneidas' claim as one for redress of a past wrong, the Court held that three doctrines – each related to the passage of time since the wrong was committed –prevent the Oneidas from obtaining the redress they seek, i.e., to be free from state and local taxation. First, the majority invoked the doctrine of laches, "a doctrine focused on one side's inaction and the other's legitimate reliance," which bars "long-dormant claims for equitable relief."[26] The Court noted that laches barred the Oneidas' claim not only because of the passage of time between the wrong committed and the claim for relief, but also because of the intervening change in the value and character of the land in question.[27]

The Court next ruled that, regardless of whether the original conveyance was lawful or not, the Oneidas had acquiesced over the last 200 years in the possession of the lands by other parties, creating reasonable expectations among surrounding communities regarding who has the right to exercise regulatory control over the lands in question. Consequently, the Court ruled, "Parcel-by-parcel revival of their sovereign status, given the extraordinary passage of time, would dishonor 'the historic wisdom of repose.'"[28]

Finally, the majority cited the doctrine of impracticality as a bar to the Oneidas' claim, holding that allowing the Oneidas to unilaterally reassert regulatory control over former reservation lands simply by repurchasing them "would have disruptive practical consequences."[29] The Court noted that both the City of Sherrill and Oneida County are "today overwhelmingly populated by non-Indians," and that ruling in favor of the Oneidas would allow tribes to unilaterally create "a checkerboard of alternating state and tribal jurisdiction in New York State."[30] The Court then pointed out that Congress had considered the practical difficulties of such an arrangement, and for that reason had created a process for taking land into trust for Indian tribes.[31] It is this statutory procedure, the Court found, that is the Oneidas' proper avenue for acquiring lands that will be free from state and local taxation.[32]

CONCLUSION

While the Supreme Court did not directly address *Cayuga Indian Nation*, the majority's opinion leaves little doubt that the Court was looking beyond state and municipal taxation to questions of general regulatory authority. As the Court put it, "If [the Oneidas] may unilaterally reassert sovereign control and remove these parcels from the local tax rolls, little would prevent the Tribe from initiating a new generation of litigation to free the parcels from local zoning or other regulatory controls that protect all landowners in the area."[33] The Court indicated the broad reach of its rationale at the very beginning of its opinion:

> Given the longstanding, distinctly non-Indian character of the area and its inhabitants, the regulatory authority constantly exercised by New York State and its counties and towns, and the Oneidas' long delay in seeking judicial relief against parties other than the United States, we hold that the Tribe cannot unilaterally revive its ancient sovereignty, in whole or in part, over the parcels at issue. The Oneidas long ago relinquished the reins of government and cannot regain them through open-market purchases from current titleholders.[34]

It is unlikely that *Cayuga Indian Nation* or any other opinion like it could stand against the weight of the Court's strong and clear direction with respect to New York tribes' attempts to reassert sovereignty over former tribal lands by merely purchasing them on the open market.

It does not appear that the ruling will have any effect on the various claims for monetary compensation springing from the Supreme Court's 1985 ruling. The

Court seemed concerned only with tribal attempts to shield newly acquired lands from state regulatory authority.

REFERENCES

[1] U.S. Const., Art. I, § 8, cl. 3.
[2] Montana v. Blackfeet Nation of Indian Tribes, 451 U.S. 759, 764 (1985).
[3] See, e.g., County of Yakima v. Confederated Tribes and Bands of Yakima Indian Nation, 502 U.S. 251, 258 (1992).
[4] 7 Stat. 44. The facts are taken from the Second Circuit's opinion in the case. See Oneida Indian Nation v. Sherrill, 337 F.3d 139, 144-146 (2d Cir. 2003) (hereinafter, "Second Circuit Opinion").
[5] 7 Stat. 45.
[6] The Indian Trade and Intercourse Act, better known today as the Nonintercourse Act, was passed in 1790 (1 Stat. 137). The current version is codified, as amended, at 25 U.S.C. § 177 ("No purchase...or other conveyance of lands...from any Indian nation or tribe of Indians, shall be of any validity in law or equity, unless the same be made by treaty or convention entered into pursuant to the Constitution.").
[7] See Indian Removal Act of 1830, 4 Stat 411.
[8] 7 Stat. 550.
[9] Id. at 554.
[10] See, e.g., New York Indians v. U.S., 170 U.S. 1 (1898); Oneida Indian Nation of New York v. County of Oneida, 414 U.S. 661 (1974).
[11] Oneida County v. Oneida Indian Nation, 470 U.S. 226 (1985).
[12] Id. at 253, note 27.
[13] See, e.g., Associated Press, *Five Land Claim Tribes Meet* (March 31, 2005). This story can be found at [http://www.gazetteextra.com/oneidas033105.asp] (Last visited, March 31, 2005).
[14] While Congress has granted the State of New York significant criminal and civil jurisdiction over tribal lands in New York, Congress specifically directed that "nothing herein contained shall be construed as subjecting the lands within any Indian reservation in the State of New York to taxation for State or local purposes." 25 U.S.C. § 233.
[15] *Oneida v. City of Sherrill*, 145 F.Supp.2d 226 (N.D.N.Y. 2001).
[16] Second Circuit Opinion, 337 F.3d at 158. On this second point, however, the court noted that, when confronted with the question of Congress's intent to disestablish a reservation or diminish reservation land, the Supreme Court

has looked to legislative history and the circumstances surrounding the treaty in question. *Id.* at 159-160.
[17] *Id.* at 162.
[18] *Id.* at 157.
[19] 317 F.Supp.2d 128 (N.D.N.Y. 2004).
[20] 25 U.S.C. §§ 2701-2721; 18 U.S.C. §§ 1168. IGRA provides the legal framework for the conduct of gaming activities on Indian lands generally free from the strictures of state and local regulation. *See generally* CRS Report RS21499, *Indian Regulatory Gaming Act: Gaming on Newly Acquired Lands*, by M. Maureen Murphy.
[21] *Cayuga Indian Nation*, 317 F.Supp.2d at 137.
[22] *Id.* at 148.
[23] *City of Sherrill v. Oneida Indian Nation of N.Y.*, 453 U.S. __ , 2005 WL 701058 (2005) (hereinafter "*Sherrill*") (slip op., at 14, note 8).
[24] *Oneida County v. Oneida Indian Nation*, 470 U.S. 226, 253, note 27 (1985).
[25] *Sherrill*, slip. op., at 13-14. The Court cast the Oneidas' claim as one for equitable relief in another portion of the majority opinion as well: "In contrast to *Oneida* I and *Oneida* II, [the Oneidas] sought equitable relief prohibiting, currently and in the future, the imposition of property taxes." *Sherrill*, slip. op. at 11.
[26] *Id.* at 17.
[27] Id.
[28] *Id.* at 19 (quoting *Oneida County v. Oneida Indian Nation*, 470 U.S. 226, 262 (1985)(Stevens, J., dissenting in part)).
[29] *Sherrill*, slip. op. at 19.
[30] *Id.* at 20.
[31] *See* 25 U.S.C. § 465.
[32] *Sherrill*, slip. op. at 21.
[33] *Id.* at 20. In his dissent, Justice Stevens intimated that the majority's fear of opening a pandora's box with respect to other regulatory issues may have motivated the Court's decision. *Id.*, Justice Stevens dissent, at 5 ("I would not decide this case on the basis of speculation about what may happen in future litigation over other regulatory issues").
[34] *Sherrill*, slip. op. at 2.

In: Native Americans: Rights, Laws...
Editor: C. P. Townsend, pp. 139-146

ISBN: 978-1-60456-202-6
© 2008 Nova Science Publishers, Inc.

Chapter 9

THE BUREAU OF INDIAN AFFAIRS' PROCESS FOR RECOGNIZING GROUPS AS INDIAN TRIBES[*]

M. Maureen Murphy

ABSTRACT

The list of federally recognized Indian tribes is not a static one. The Department of the Interior's Bureau of Indian Affairs has an administrative process by which a group may establish itself as an Indian tribe and become eligible for the services and benefits accorded Indian tribes under federal law. The process requires extensive documentation, including verification of continuous existence as an Indian tribe since 1900, and generally takes considerable time. Final determinations are subject to judicial review.

FEDERAL RECOGNITION OR ACKNOWLEDGMENT OF INDIAN TRIBAL EXISTENCE

The list of federally recognized Indian tribes is not static. Not only does Congress periodically pass legislation according federal recognition to individual tribes, but the Department of the Interior (DOI), through its Bureau of Indian

---

[*] Excerpted from CRS Report RS21109, dated March 25, 2005.

Affairs (BIA) has a process, 25 C.F.R. Part 83, by which a group can establish itself as an Indian tribe and thereby become eligible for all the services and benefits accorded to Indian tribes under federal law.[1] Included among these are the ability to have land taken into trust under 25 C.F.R. Part 151 and to conduct gaming under the Indian Gaming Regulatory Act, 25 U.S.C. §§ 2701, *et seq.* As of November 16, 2001, there were approximately 212 groups petitioning under this process, including 186 that were not ready for evaluation.

THE ADMINISTRATIVE RECOGNITION PROCESS

DOI regulations, 25 C.F.R. § 83.7, include seven mandatory criteria. For each of these, the petitioning group must establish "a reasonable likelihood of the validity of the facts relating to that criterion." 25 C.F.R. § 83.6(d).

- Existence as an Indian tribe on a continuous basis since 1900. Evidence may include documents showing that governmental authorities —federal, state, or local — have identified it as an Indian group; identification by anthropologists and scholars; and evidence from newspapers and books.
- Existence predominantly as a community. This may be established by geographical residence of 50% of the group; marriage patterns; kinship and language patterns; cultural patterns; and social or religious patterns.
- Political influence or authority over members as an autonomous entity from historical times until the present. This may be established by showing evidence of leaders' ability to mobilize the group or settle disputes, inter-group communication links, and active political processes.
- Copies of its governing documents and membership criteria.
- Evidence that the membership descends from an historical tribe or tribes that combined and functioned together as a political entity. This may be established by tribal rolls, federal or state records, church or school records, affidavits of leaders and members, and other records.
- Unless unusual circumstances exist, evidence that most of the group's members do not belong to any other acknowledged North American tribe.
- Absence of federal legislation barring recognition.

TIME LINE FOR HANDLING PETITIONS BY GROUPS SEEKING INDIAN TRIBAL STATUS

- Group presents petition to BIA.
- BIA must acknowledge receipt of letter of intent or petition within 30 days. It must issue a *Federal Register* notice within 60 days. This acts as a notice to interested parties to submit factual or legal arguments in support of or opposing the petition. Notice is also to be supplied to the governor and attorney general of the state in which the group is located.
- BIA conducts a technical assistance review and informs the petitioner as to supplemental material needed. Petitioner may withdraw petition or supply needed material. No time frame is given for this stage of the process. If BIA finds that petition clearly does not meet certain mandatory criteria, it may deny petition and issue *Federal Register* notice.
- When the BIA determines that the petition is ready for active consideration, it informs the petitioner. No time frame is given.
- When active consideration begins, the petitioner and interested parties are notified of the names of researchers and their supervisors. No time frame specified for beginning active consideration.
- Proposed findings must be published in the *Federal Register* a year after active consideration has begun. But active consideration may be suspended for administrative reasons or petition problems.
- After proposed findings are published, supporters or opponents have 180 days to submit arguments in support or in opposition, with the possibility of a 180-day extension. During the period, the Assistant Secretary for Indian Affairs, upon request, may hold a formal meeting to inquire into the basis for the proposed finding.
- After the expiration of the comment period and any extension, the petitioner has a minimum of 60 days to respond, and time may be extended by the Assistant Secretary. Thereafter, the Assistant Secretary has the discretion to solicit comments from the petitioner or interested parties, but no unsolicited comments will be accepted. The petitioner and interested parties will be informed of any extension of the comment or response periods.
- When the comment period has expired, the Assistant Secretary will consult with the petitioner and interested parties to determine a time frame for considering evidence and arguments.

- A final determination must be published in the *Federal Register* within 60 days after consideration has begun unless there has been extension by the Assistant Secretary. The determination must be published in the *Federal Register*. Petitioner and interested parties must be notified of any extension of the 60 days.
- Determination is effective 90 days after publication unless the petitioner or an interested party files a request for reconsideration with the Interior Board of Indian Appeals (Board) under 25 C.F.R. § 83.11. To vacate the determination, the petitioner or interested party must prove by the preponderance of the evidence: (1) that there is new evidence that could affect the determination; (2) that a substantial part of the evidence reliedupon was unreliable; (3) that the petitioner's or the BIA's research was inadequate in a material respect; or (4) that reasonable alternative interpretations, not considered, would affect the determination. 25 C.F.R. § 83.11(d)(1)-(4).
- The Board may either affirm the determination or vacate it and remand it to the Assistant Secretary for reconsideration. Under certain circumstances, it may affirm the determination but send it to the Secretary for reconsideration.
- If the determination has been sent to the Secretary for reconsideration, the petitioner and interested parties have 30 days to submit comments. If an interested party opposing a petition submits comments, the petitioner shall have 15 days, after receipt of comments, to respond.
- The Secretary must make a determination within 60 days of receipt of all comments. If the Secretary decides against reconsideration, the decision becomes effective when all parties are notified.
- If the determination has been remanded to the Assistant Secretary, a reconsidered determination must be issued within 120 days of receipt of the Board's decision. The reconsidered determination is effective when notice is published in the *Federal Register*.
- Upon final agency action, a challenge may be raised in a federal district court under the judicial review provision of the Federal Administrative Procedure Act, 5 U.S.C. § 702.

PROPOSED LEGISLATION

Congress has considered replacing the administrative recognition process by a statute to be administered outside of BIA. H.Rept. 105-737, 105th Cong, 2d Sess.

(1998), saw the current administrative process as poorly funded, too protracted, and deficient in due process. Costs per tribe can run to $500,000; the average year sees the completion of only 1.3 petitions; and sometimes the very people who search out the facts of a case craft the decision. A GAO Report, *Indian Issues: Improvements Needed in Tribal Recognition Process* (November 2001), recommended that DOI improve its responsiveness and develop transparent guidelines for interpreting the main criteria under the recognition procedures. Three 107th Congress bills, S. 504, S. 1392, and H.R. 1175, would have provided a statutory recognition process. Another, S. 1393, would have authorized grants for petitioning groups and local government participation. Other bills recognize specific groups as Indian tribes.

In the 108th Congress, two bills would have established a statutory framework for an administrative acknowledgment process by which an Indian group or tribe could petition DOI for recognition as an Indian tribe: S. 462 and S. 297. Another, S. 463, would have authorized grants for petitioning groups and local government participation in the administrative acknowledgment process.

In the 109th Congress, there have been several bills, including:

- H.R. 309 would establish a process by which a Native Hawaiian governmental entity may be recognized by the United States. Specifically excluded from any powers conferred is the right to conduct gaming under IGRA or be eligible for any BIA programs and services not otherwise available.
- H.R. 464 would establish an independent Commission on Indian Recognition, which is to operate for eight years, to adjudicate petitions by groups seeking recognition as Indian tribes. The bill would withdraw existing BIA authority to recognize groups as Indian tribes and require it to transfer all pending petitions to the Commission. The legislation would set procedures, including deadlines, for the Commission's handling of petitions and for according recognition. Included are: identification by at least one specified governmental or other entity, as an Indian group; existence as a community from historical times to the present; political influence and autonomy; governing documents; and, membership rolls. There are provisions making available to petitioners certain procedural rights in any adjudicatory hearing and the authority to bring an enforcement action in federal court.
- H.R. 512 would, if a group requested it, require the Secretary to meet an expedited schedule for issuing proposed findings and final determinations for groups that have made an initial application before October 17, 1988,

and were listed as "Ready, Waiting for Active Consideration" on July 1, 2004. It also would provide petitioners a means of judicial adjudication should the Secretary fail to meet the established deadlines as well as judicial review of an adverse determination.
- H.R. 852 would extend recognition to the Duwamish Tribe; establish its service area; and, require the Secretary to take into trust any fee land, in the service area or the Tribe's aboriginal homelands, which is transferred by the Tribe to the Secretary within 10 years of enactment.
- H.R. 1354 would specify that federal acknowledgment is not to be granted to any group unless it has met all criteria in 25 C.F.R., Part 83, in effect on January 1, 2004. It would require the Secretary, in issuing any proposed findings, to publish in the *Federal Register* detailed findings on the application of each of the criteria.
- S. 437 would set a date by which the Secretary must review the petition of the Grand River Band of Ottawa Indians and submit detailed findings with respect to certain questions relating to the history of the Band. Failure to submit such a report would require the Secretary to recognize the Band as an Indian tribe. There is also a provision reaffirming any rights of the Band that have previously been abrogated or diminished.
- S. 480 would provide federal recognition to six tribes of Virginia, require the Secretary to take land in specified counties in trust as a reservation for each of the tribes should such land be transferred to the Secretary for that purpose; and specifies that some of the exceptions to the Indian Gaming Regulatory Act's (IGRA) prohibition on gaming on lands acquired after October 17, 1988, would not be available to the tribes. It does not eliminate the exception under 25 U.S.C. § 2719(b)(1)(A), which requires the Secretary to make a two-part determination that gaming on the land would be in the best interest of the tribe and not detrimental to the local community in which the governor of the state concurs. Nor does it eliminate the other requirements under IGRA, including a tribal-state compact for casino gaming.
- S. 630 would establish a statutory framework for an administrative acknowledgment process by which an Indian group or tribe could petition DOI for recognition as an Indian tribe with a government-to-government relationship with the United States and members entitled to federal services to Indians. The bill sets standards for eligibility that generally deny eligibility to: groups formed after December 31, 2002, for the purpose of seeking acknowledgment; groups separating from an existing federally recognized Indian tribe; terminated tribes; and groups whose

petition for acknowledgment had previously been denied by DOI. Among the mandatory criteria for acknowledgment in this legislation are: identification as an Indian group on a substantially continuous basis since 1900; existence of a distinct community comprised of a predominant portion of the membership since 1900; maintenance of political influence as an autonomous authority over members since 1900; evidence of governing documents and membership criteria; list with addresses of current members; evidence that members are not members of other Indian tribes; and, evidence that there has been no federal termination of tribal existence or prohibition on acknowledging the group.

REFERENCES

[1] The federal courts have had a role in determining whether a group qualifies as an Indian tribe for a particular purpose. For example, in 1877, in *United States v. Joseph*, 94 U.S. 614, the Supreme Court determined that the Pueblos were not an Indian tribe for purposes of the Indian liquor laws. Later, their status was reconsidered, and the Pueblos were held to be an Indian tribe and their lands protected under a federal law that prohibited the sale or alienation of Indian land without federal approval. *United States v. Candelaria*, 231 U.S. 28 (1913). Groups have sought court orders to compel DOI to process their applications for acknowledgment in a more timely fashion. See, e.g., *Tribe v. Babbitt*, 233 F. Supp. 2d 30 (D.D.C. 2000). That approach may have been precluded by a ruling in *Mashpee Wapanoag Tribal Council, Inc. v. Norton*, 336 F. 3d 1094 (D.C. Cir. 2003), in favor of DOI. The court found that competing agency priorities and limited resources must be considered in claims that the length of time it takes to process an acknowledgment petition is unreasonable within the meaning of the Administrative Procedure Act. 5 U.S.C. § 555(b). Other groups have tried the indirect approach of identifying a statute that requires that the plaintiff be an Indian tribe and suing under that statute in an attempt to force a court to determine whether that particular statute's definition of "Indian tribe" has been met. In *Golden Hill Paugusset Tribe of Indians v. Weicker*, 39 F. 3d 51 (2d Cir. 1994), involving a land claim by a group asserting that it is an Indian tribe and its land had been alienated without federal approval in violation of 25 U.S.C. § 177, the court remanded the case to the district court with instructions to enjoin the litigation for 18 months pending DOI resolution of the group's acknowledgment petition. In *New York v.*

Shinnecock Indian Nation, 280 F. Supp. 2d 1 (E.D. N.Y. 2003), the court temporarily enjoined a state-recognized tribe's construction of a gaming operation for 18 months pending DOI action on an acknowledgment petition. Both courts saw DOI's jurisdiction over the question as primary and their court's jurisdiction as secondary and seemed to have indicated that the court would take up the issue of tribal existence in the absence of a ruling by DOI.

In: Native Americans: Rights, Laws... ISBN: 978-1-60456-202-6
Editor: C. P. Townsend, pp. 147-154 © 2008 Nova Science Publishers, Inc.

Chapter 10

APPLICATION OF CAMPAIGN FINANCE LAW TO INDIAN TRIBES[*]

L. Paige Whitaker and Joseph E. Cantor

ABSTRACT

Under the Federal Election Campaign Act (FECA), Indian tribes are subject to contribution limits applicable to "persons," as defined by the act. For the 2008 election cycle, these limits include $2,300 per election to a candidate, $28,500 per year to a political party's national committee, and $5,000 per year to a political action committee (PAC). The Federal Election Commission (FEC) has found, however, that FECA's $108,200 election cycle aggregate limit applicable to "individuals," as defined by the act, does not apply to Indian tribes (similar to FECA's treatment of other interest groups that operate through PACs and are also not subject to an aggregate limit). In addition, as most Indian tribes are unincorporated, they are not subject to the FECA ban on use of corporate treasury funds for contributions and expenditures in connection with federal elections. Hence, unlike corporations, most Indian tribes are not required to establish PACs in order to participate in federal elections. As the result of an FEC ruling, unlike PACs, Indian tribes are also not required to disclose the amounts and recipients of any contributions they make. With regard to unregulated soft money, Indian tribes may spend unlimited amounts of money on issue advocacy communications.

---

[*] Excerpted from CRS Report RS21176, dated January 25, 2007.

The Bipartisan Campaign Reform Act (BCRA) of 2002 made several significant changes to FECA, including increasing certain contribution limits from their previous levels. BCRA also prohibited any "person," which includes Indian tribes, from making soft money donations to political parties. While FECA prohibits corporations and unions from paying for broadcast issue advertisements that refer to federal candidates within 30 days of a primary or 60 days of a general election, labeled by BCRA as "electioneering communications," unincorporated Indian tribes are not subject to such a prohibition. However, if an Indian tribe sponsors an electioneering communication, regardless of its incorporation status, it is subject to disclosure requirements, including the identification of disbursements and donors over certain dollar amounts.

APPLICATION OF CAMPAIGN FINANCE LAW TO INDIAN TRIBES

Activity Fully Regulated by Federal Law: Hard Money

The Federal Election Campaign Act (FECA)[1] regulates contributions and expenditures for federal election campaigns. The term "hard money," which is not statutorily defined, typically refers to funds raised and spent in accordance with the limitations, prohibitions, and reporting requirements of FECA.[2] Unlike soft money, which will be discussed in the next section, hard money may be used "in connection with" or "for the purpose of influencing" federal elections.

Under FECA, hard money restrictions apply to contributions from and expenditures by any "person," as defined to include "an individual, partnership, committee, association, corporation, labor organization, or any other organization or group of persons," but not including the federal government.[3] FECA provides that a "person" is limited to contributing no more than

- $2,000 per candidate, per election[4] (adjusted for inflation to $2,300 for the 2007-2008 election cycle);
- $25,000 per year to a national committee of a political party[5] (adjusted for inflation to $28,500 for the 2007-2008 election cycle); and
- $5,000 per year to PACs[6] (limits on contributions by and to PACs are not adjusted for inflation).

FECA further provides that an "individual" is subject to an aggregate limit on all contributions per two-year election cycle (encompassing all contributions to federally registered candidates, parties, and PACs): $95,000 per two-year election cycle, with sub-limits: (a) $37,500 to all candidates and (b) $57,500 to all PACs and parties (no more than $37,500 of which is to state and local parties and PACs).[7] As indexed for inflation, the 2007-2008 election cycle limit is $108,200, with sub-limits: (a) $42,700 to all candidates and (b) $65,500 to all PACs and parties (no more than $42,700 of which is to state and local parties and PACs).

In interpreting such statutory provisions, the Federal Election Commission (FEC) has consistently found that the act's definition of "person" includes unincorporated Indian tribes, thereby subjecting tribes to the $2,300 per candidate per election limit, the $28,500 per year limit to a national party, and the $5,000 per year limit to PACs.[8] On May 15, 2000, however, the FEC found that whereas an unincorporated Indian tribe is considered a "person" under FECA, it is not considered an "individual" and therefore is not subject to the aggregate election-cycle limit.[9] As a result of that ruling, it appears that an Indian tribe, by making, for example, an unlimited number of $2,300, $28,500, and $5,000 contributions, could significantly exceed the $108,200 aggregate election-cycle limit applicable to "individuals."[10]

FECA also prohibits corporations, labor unions, and national banks from using their treasury funds to make contributions and expenditures in connection with federal elections.[11] Such entities may, however, participate in financing federal elections by establishing separate segregated funds, also known as political action committees (PACs), which are permitted to raise voluntary contributions for use in federal elections.[12] PAC contributions are subject to limitations under FECA, as are contributions from individual citizens and political parties.

Generally, as most Indian tribes are unincorporated, they are not subject to the FECA ban on the use of corporate treasury funds for contributions and expenditures in connection with federal elections. Accordingly, most tribes may make contributions in federal elections directly from their tribal funds, without establishing a PAC. This appears to facilitate the ability of Indian tribes to make federal election contributions. That is, while current law limits contributions to a PAC to $5,000 per year from any source,[13] a tribe may acquire a large amount of funds for use in federal elections more directly (i.e., from its own tribal funds, including, for example, income from tribal enterprises, so long as those enterprises are neither incorporated nor government contractors).

In one key respect, the FEC treats Indian tribes differently than PACs. Although a 1978 FEC ruling had required Indian tribes making contributions to comply with the periodic reporting requirements of FECA,[14] this requirement was explicitly superceded by a 1995 agency ruling.[15] Although contributions from tribes must be reported by recipients, one must view the FEC filings of candidates, PACs, and parties in order to track the funds given by an Indian tribe, as well as the IRS filings by section 527 political organizations. *PoliticalMoneyLine* found that some $25 million was donated for 2000-20005 federal elections by 212 federally recognized Indian tribes, and that the reporting was made under almost 2,000 different variations of their names.[16] Thus, the ability to track the flow of election-related money from Indian tribes is more difficult than it is for other large entities.

Several observations may be made about the ability of Indian tribes to spend money in federal elections compared with that of other interest groups, which typically operate through PACs. Like other interest groups, Indian tribes are subject to no aggregate limit on their total federal election contributions (only individual citizens are subject to this limit). Unlike an interest group PAC, however, an Indian tribe may have a more readily available pool of funds that could be used in federal elections, that is, its own tribal funds, as opposed to a fund solely comprised of contributions that are subject to limitations and source restrictions. This advantage, however, may be somewhat offset by the $5,000 per candidate, per election limit applicable to a PAC, which typically qualifies as a "multicandidate committee,"[17] compared with the $2,300 per candidate, per election limit applicable to all other persons, including Indian tribes. (In one apparent anomaly in FECA, a multicandidate committee may only contribute $15,000 per year to the national committee of a political party, whereas any other person, including an Indian tribe, may contribute $25,000,[18] or $28,500 in the 2007-2008 election cycle, adjusted for inflation.)

Activity Not Fully Regulated by Federal Law: Soft Money

While "soft money" is not expressly defined in federal election law and regulation, strictly speaking, it refers to funds that are not regulated by FECA (i.e., hard money). It may refer to corporate and labor treasury funds that cannot legally be used in connection with federal elections, but can be used for other specified purposes. Sometimes referred to as nonfederal funds, prior to the enactment of the Bipartisan Campaign Reform Act (BCRA) of 2002 (P.L. 107-155; March 27, 2002), "soft money" often referred to non-FECA funds raised by the national committees of the two major political parties. BCRA put an end to this practice by prohibiting national parties from raising funds not subject to FECA, whether from individual citizens, corporations, labor unions, or Indian tribes.[19]

Application of Campaign Finance Law to Indian Tribes   151

Treatment of Indian Tribes Versus Most Interest Groups and Individual Citizens under Federal Election Law

Individual Citizens	Indian Tribes	Most Interest Groups
	HARD MONEY	
	Contributions	
• $2,300 to a candidate* • $28,500 to national party* • Aggregate limit per 2-year election cycle: $108,200, with various sub-limits**	*Treated as persons:* • $2,300 to a candidate* • $28,500 to national party* • No aggregate limit per election cycle	*Activity through PACs:* • $5,000 to a candidate • $15,000 to a national party • No aggregate limit per election cycle
	Receipts (sources of funds used for contributions)	
Personal funds of individuals who are U.S. citizens or permanent resident aliens	Tribal funds (but may contain no funds from incorporated businesses or government contractors)	Only amounts donated to the PAC ($5,000 per year from an individual)
	Disclosure	
Individuals have no reporting requirements for contributions made, under FECA	As nonpolitical committees, Tribes have no filing requirements, per FEC ruling	PACs are required by FECA to register and submit periodic reports of receipts and expenditures
	SOFT MONEY	
Permitted to run "electioneering communications," but must disclose amounts spent	Issue Ads Permitted to run "electioneering communications" (as Indian tribes are unincorporated entities), but must disclose amounts spent and $1000+ donors	No corporate- or union-funded electioneering ads (broadcast within last 30/60 days before primary/general elections)
	Donations to Parties	
N/A (individuals may contribute to extent permitted by FECA, subject to per committee and aggregate cycle limits)	BCRA prohibited soft money (i.e., unlimited) donations to a party committee	BCRA prohibited soft money (i.e., unlimited) donations to a party committee

* Under BCRA, these limits are required to be adjusted for inflation at the start of each election cycle. The amounts shown here are the limits set for the 2007-2008 election cycle.

** Individual citizens, in contrast with Indian tribes and other interest groups via their PACs, are subject to an aggregate limit on all contributions to federal candidates, PACs, and parties (through federal accounts), currently $108,200 per two-year cycle, with sub-limits: (a) $42,700 to all candidates; and (b) $65,500 to all PACs and parties (no more than $42,700 of which is to state and local parties and PACs), all indexed.

Even after the enactment of BCRA, however, spending on issue advocacy communications remains a prominent soft money activity. Issue advocacy communications are generally paid for by a group, such as a for-profit or nonprofit corporation or labor union, for advertisements (typically broadcast on radio or television) that could be interpreted to favor or disfavor certain candidates, while also serving to inform the public about a policy issue. Prior to BCRA, issue advocacy communications were generally unregulated by FECA.[20] Therefore, Indian tribes (like corporations, labor unions, and individuals) could spend unlimited amounts of money on such communications.

With the enactment of BCRA, *certain* issue ads are now regulated. BCRA created a new term in federal election law, "electioneering communication," which describes a political ad that "refers" to a clearly identified federal candidate, is broadcast within 30 days of a primary or 60 days of a general election, and if for House and Senate elections, is "targeted to the relevant electorate," (i.e., is received by 50,000 or more persons in the state or district where the respective House or Senate election is occurring).[21] BCRA prohibits the financing of such communications with union or certain corporate funds.[22] Furthermore, for permissible "electioneering communications," federal election law requires disclosure of disbursements over $10,000 for such communications, including identification of each donor of $1,000 or more.[23] Therefore, while corporations and labor unions are prohibited from engaging in "electioneering communications," it appears that most Indian tribes, as unincorporated entities, may continue to finance such communications, subject to the disclosure requirements.

REFERENCES

[1] 2 U.S.C. § 431 *et seq.*
[2] *See* 2 U.S.C. §§ 441a, 441b(a).
[3] 2 U.S.C. § 431(11).
[4] 2 U.S.C. § 441a(a)(1)(A).
[5] 2 U.S.C. § 441a(a)(1)(B).
[6] 2 U.S.C. § 441a(a)(1)(C).
[7] 2 U.S.C. § 441a(a)(3).
[8] *See* Federal Election Commission Advisory Opinion, AO 2000-05 (May 15, 2000), *citing* AO 1978-51, 1999-32, and 1993-12 (where the Commission found that, as "persons," unincorporated Indian tribes were subject to the prohibition on contributions by persons with Federal contracts if they are engaged in such contracts).

[9] Federal Election Commission Advisory Opinion, AO 2000-05 (May 15, 2000).
[10] For example, one commentator estimated that without the aggregate limit, an Indian tribe in 2000 could contribute: $240,000 during a two-year election cycle to the two major national parties and their affiliated House and Senate campaign committees; up to $1 million during an election cycle to the 100 state party committees; and distribute as much as $1,872,000 to every candidate running for the House and Senate from the two major political parties. Edward Zuckerman, *FEC Lets Indian Tribes Convert Government Funds to Political Contributions*, Political Finance and Lobby Reporter, vol. 21, June 14, 2000.
[11] 2 U.S.C. § 441b(a).
[12] 2 U.S.C. § 441b(b)(2)(C).
[13] 2 U.S.C. § 441a(a)(1)(C).
[14] Federal Election Commission Advisory Opinion, AO 1978-51 (Sept. 1, 1978).
[15] Federal Election Commission Advisory Opinion, AO 1995-11 (Apr. 28, 1995), footnote 10.
[16] *PoliticalMoneyLine* Home Page Update, Jan. 28, 2006.
[17] 2 U.S.C. § 441a(a)(2)(A). A multicandidate committee is defined in 2 U.S.C. § 441a(a)(4) as a political committee that has been registered for at least six months, has received contributions from more than 50 persons, and, except for state party committees, has made contributions to five or more federal candidates.
[18] 2 U.S.C. §§ 441a(a)(2)(B), 441a(a)(1)(B).
[19] 2 U.S.C. § 441i(a).
[20] Prior to the Supreme Court upholding the constitutionality of BCRA's regulation of electioneering communications in *McConnell v. FEC*, 540 U.S. 93 (2003), the prevailing view of the U.S. appellate courts was that Supreme Court precedent (specifically, *Buckley v. Valeo*, 424 U.S. 1 (1976)) mandated that a communication contain *express* words advocating the election or defeat of a clearly identified candidate in order for it to be constitutionally regulated. If a communication did not contain such express words, most courts determined that it could not be regulated. Effectively overturning such lower court rulings, the Supreme Court in *McConnell* held that neither the First Amendment nor *Buckley* prohibits BCRA's regulation of "electioneering communications," even though electioneering communications, by definition, do not necessarily contain express advocacy. The Court determined that when the *Buckley* Court distinguished

between express and issue advocacy, it did so as a matter of statutory interpretation, not constitutional command. Moreover, the Court announced that, by narrowly reading the FECA provisions in *Buckley* to avoid problems of vagueness and overbreadth, it "did not suggest that a statute that was neither vague nor overbroad would be required to toe the same express advocacy line." McConnell, 540 U.S. at 189-194.

[21] 2 U.S.C. §§434(f)(3)(A), (C).

[22] 2 U.S.C. §441b(b)(2). This prohibition does not appear to apply to broadcast ads that would otherwise be considered "electioneering communications" under BCRA, if they are paid for by Internal Revenue Code (IRC) §527 or §501(c) organizations that are unincorporated. Although 2 U.S.C. §441b(c)(2) exempts from the prohibition IRC §527 and §501(c)(4) corporations that pay for ads exclusively with funds provided by individuals who are U.S. citizens or nationals or who are lawfully admitted for permanent residence, §441b(c)(6) subsequently appears to nullify that exemption by providing that the exception does not apply if the communication is "targeted."

[23] 2 U.S.C. §434(f).

INDEX

A

AC, xii, 147
access, viii, 6, 9, 25, 27, 30, 32, 39, 41, 51, 52, 54, 77
accidents, 9, 38
accounting, 103, 104
ADA, 25
administration, 20, 54, 55, 92
administrators, 105
adults, 9, 39
advertisements, xii, 148, 152
advocacy, 45, 151, 153
age, 12, 79, 80, 81, 112
agriculture, 57, 58, 59
Alaska, vii, 2, 3, 5, 16, 20, 25, 31, 45, 47, 85, 108, 117
Alaskan Native(s), vii, 1, 25, 45, 47, 108
alcohol, 9, 23, 32, 33, 38, 39
alcohol abuse, 9, 39
alcoholism, 3, 9, 38
alienation, 122, 145
alternative, 122, 123, 142
amendments, 22, 30, 36, 41, 48, 83
American culture, 58
American Indian(s), vii, 1, 2, 20, 41, 42, 45, 65, 67, 69, 77, 80, 81, 82, 86, 103, 108
amputation, 9
AN, vii, 1, 2, 3, 6, 8, 9, 10, 12, 13, 18, 20, 26, 35, 38, 41, 42
Ancient One, ix, 71, 73, 86
Archaeological Resources Protection Act, 76, 82
argument, 82, 96, 133, 134
Arizona, 3, 7, 31, 52, 56, 57, 59, 60, 62, 63, 64, 66, 67, 69, 127
armed forces, 108
Army Corps of Engineers ("COE"), ix, 71, 73, 79
assessment, 78
assets, 103, 104, 105
Attorney General, 78
auditing, 39
authority, viii, 2, 3, 4, 6, 13, 15, 19, 20, 26, 27, 29, 34, 40, 41, 43, 61, 78, 79, 106, 107, 108, 117, 123, 127, 132, 136, 137, 140, 143, 145
autonomy, 108, 143
availability, 37, 55, 57, 83, 91, 94, 96, 97
avoidance, 55

B

Balanced Budget Act, 12, 15
banking, 122
banks, 149
barriers, 78
benefits, xii, 15, 29, 31, 35, 36, 125, 139, 140

binding, 95, 96
Bipartisan Campaign Reform Act (BCRA), xii, 148, 150
birth, viii, 1, 7, 8, 9, 114
births, 12
blindness, 9
blood, 12, 13
blood pressure, 13
blood supply, 12
brain, 12
Bureau of Land Management, 126
Bureau of the Census, 11
Bush Administration, 88

C

California, 3, 33, 56, 59, 64, 66, 67, 126
campaigns, 148
cancer, 12
candidates, xii, 148, 149, 150, 151, 152, 153
CAP, 52
cardiovascular disease, 9
case law, 61
cast, 138
casting, 135
Census, 8, 10, 11
Census Bureau, 10, 11
certainty, 56
certification, 37, 76
Cheyenne, 70
children, x, 7, 8, 37, 48, 111, 112, 113, 114, 115, 117, 119
cholesterol, 13
civil action, 78
Civil War, 19
classes, 122
codes, 61, 68
colleges, 24
commerce, 107
common law, 65
communication, xii, 10, 140, 148, 152, 153, 154
community, 6, 7, 23, 24, 25, 28, 33, 108, 117, 124, 125, 140, 143, 145
compensation, 40, 136

compliance, 31, 36, 80, 81, 91, 104
complications, 26
components, 112
conditioning, 91
Confederated Tribes of the Grand Ronde Community of Oregon, 126
conflict, 53, 61, 65, 91
conflict of interest, 53
confusion, 55, 56, 61
Congress, viii, ix, x, xi, 2, 3, 4, 7, 12, 14, 15, 18, 19, 20, 21, 22, 26, 27, 31, 34, 35, 37, 38, 39, 40, 41, 42, 43, 44, 45, 46, 47, 49, 51, 52, 53, 54, 58, 59, 63, 65, 68, 69, 72, 78, 82, 83, 84, 90, 91, 92, 93, 94, 95, 96, 97, 101, 102, 103, 104, 106, 107, 108, 111, 112, 113, 117, 123, 126, 132, 133, 134, 136, 137, 139, 142, 143
Congressional Budget Office (CBO), 14, 30, 48
Congressional Research Service, (CRS), xi, 1, 5, 10, 14, 17, 42, 44, 45, 46, 48, 51, 71, 89, 101, 102, 105, 107, 109, 111, 121, 128, 131, 138, 139, 147
Connecticut, 127
consensus, 28
consent, 54, 55, 76, 115, 123, 124, 127, 132
conservation, 19
consolidation, 39
Constitution, 3, 53, 96, 108, 132, 137
constraints, 34
construction, x, 6, 23, 27, 28, 32, 40, 46, 57, 74, 76, 101, 102, 114, 123, 134, 146
consultants, 13, 18
consulting, 125
control, x, 13, 20, 26, 27, 32, 60, 72, 74, 76, 77, 78, 82, 87, 90, 91, 112, 135, 136
corporations, xii, 67, 147, 148, 149, 150, 152, 154
costs, viii, x, 2, 21, 37, 38, 46, 48, 89, 90, 91, 95, 97, 104, 125
counsel, 116
Court of Appeals, ix, 72, 73, 81, 88, 92, 104, 133
coverage, 18, 26, 46, 84, 107
covering, x, 26, 28, 33, 101, 103

credit, 113
crime, 113
criticism, 40
crops, 56
cultural connections, 125
culture, ix, 57, 72, 73, 75, 81, 82, 84, 86, 112
curiosity, 73
currency, vii

D

data gathering, 103
data processing, 37
dating, 79, 80
death(s), viii, 1, 8, 9, 12, 86
death rate, 8, 12
debt, 123
decisions, x, 3, 33, 80, 81, 82, 89, 112, 114, 119, 125
defects, 40
defendants, 81, 83, 87
definition, 23, 24, 55, 65, 73, 75, 82, 83, 84, 85, 124, 145, 149, 153
deflate, 45
delivery, vii, 1, 2, 3, 5, 6, 7, 23, 26, 28, 34, 35, 36, 37, 43
demand, 23, 117
demographic characteristics, 15
denial, 127
dentists, 6, 25
Department of Health and Human Services, vii, 1, 2, 10, 17, 43, 44, 45, 46, 49, 90, 102
Department of Housing and Urban Development (HUD), 27
Department of the Interior, xi, 11, 40, 45, 47, 61, 65, 83, 90, 97, 114, 121, 123, 139
desire, 63
diabetes, 3, 9, 13, 15, 26, 32, 45
dialysis, 26
diamond, 88
direct costs, 37
disclosure, xii, 148, 152
discrimination, 108
disorder, 33

disposition, ix, 71, 72, 73, 74, 75, 78, 79, 81, 85, 88
distribution, 3, 58
District of Columbia, 103
diversity, 57
division, 40, 41
divorce, 113
doctors, 39, 40
donations, xii, 148, 151
donors, xii, 148, 151
draft, 57
drinking water, 67
drugs, 6, 38
due process, 143
duties, 54, 65, 78, 103, 105, 107

E

economic development, x, 101, 106
economic security, 61
education, x, 4, 5, 13, 16, 19, 20, 21, 25, 33, 37, 41, 45, 48, 89, 90, 101
educational institutions, 74
educational programs, 24
election, xii, 147, 148, 149, 150, 151, 152, 153
eligibility criteria, 35
employees, 18, 24, 40, 46
employment, 15
energy, x, 45, 101
Energy and Commerce Committee, 21, 22
enrollment, 8, 10, 30, 31, 44
environment, 22, 24
equipment, 18, 26, 32, 37
equity, 137
estimating, 18
ethnic groups, vii
evidence, 38, 56, 65, 77, 78, 82, 83, 116, 140, 141, 142, 145
exclusion, 31
exercise, 68, 115, 123, 135
expenditures, xii, 15, 31, 94, 97, 147, 148, 149, 151

F

FAD, 33
failure, 38, 65, 69, 87, 94
faith, 76, 113
family, 115, 116, 118, 119
family members, 116
FDI, 18, 46
fear, 52, 138
federal courts, 54, 85, 122, 145
Federal District Court, 65
Federal Election Campaign Act, xii, 147, 148
Federal Election Commission, xii, 147, 149, 152, 153
Federal Election Commission (FEC), xii
federal elections, xii, 147, 148, 149, 150
federal funds, 48, 74
federal government, vii, x, 2, 3, 7, 34, 39, 40, 48, 52, 54, 56, 67, 76, 78, 89, 90, 92, 95, 103, 107, 132, 133, 134, 148
federal grants, 72
federal law, xii, 7, 34, 127, 134, 139, 140, 145
Federal Register, 28, 34, 77, 141, 142, 144
females, 12
fetal alcohol syndrome, 3
finance, 152
financial resources, 6, 38, 83
financing, 149, 152
First Amendment, 153
fish, 64
flexibility, 59
foreclosure, 123
fulfillment, 42
funding, viii, 2, 3, 5, 6, 13, 14, 15, 18, 20, 24, 26, 27, 28, 32, 34, 37, 38, 39, 40, 48, 90, 91, 94, 97, 104
funds, vii, viii, xii, 1, 2, 4, 5, 6, 19, 20, 22, 27, 28, 34, 37, 39, 41, 91, 92, 93, 94, 95, 96, 97, 102, 103, 105, 147, 148, 149, 150, 151, 152, 154

G

gambling, x, 101, 106, 134

General Accounting Office (GAO), 48, 143
gastroenteritis, 9
general election, xii, 148, 151, 152
generation, 136
geography, 57, 60, 108
girls, 114
glucose, 13
goals, xi, 20, 57, 63, 111
governance, 4, 6, 20, 21, 36, 37, 39, 41, 90
government, vii, x, 20, 34, 35, 53, 54, 62, 69, 76, 78, 88, 89, 90, 91, 93, 95, 96, 98, 99, 128, 132, 136, 144, 149, 151
government budget, 34
government procurement, 95, 96
GPO, 41, 42, 43, 44, 46, 47, 49
grants, 5, 15, 32, 33, 43, 55, 78, 91, 143
groundwater, 57, 62, 65, 69
groups, ix, 7, 28, 72, 73, 74, 75, 76, 85, 86, 108, 124, 140, 143, 144, 145, 150
guardian, 113
guidance, 52
guidelines, 143

H

harm, x, 106, 111, 113
Hawaii, 85, 107, 108
healing, 24
health, vii, viii, x, 1, 2, 3, 4, 5, 6, 7, 9, 12, 13, 14, 15, 18, 19, 20, 21, 22, 23, 24, 25, 26, 27, 28, 29, 30, 31, 32, 33, 34, 35, 36, 37, 38, 39, 40, 41, 42, 43, 44, 46, 61, 101, 102
Health and Human Services (HHS), vii, viii, 1, 2, 17, 19, 21, 22, 23, 24, 26, 28, 32, 33, 34, 36, 39, 41, 43, 46, 90, 92, 94, 97, 102
health care, vii, x, 1, 3, 4, 5, 6, 9, 15, 18, 19, 20, 21, 23, 24, 25, 26, 27, 28, 29, 30, 31, 32, 34, 35, 39, 40, 101, 102
health care system, 18
health education, 26
health insurance, 15, 102
health problems, 3, 33, 38, 40, 41
health services, viii, 1, 2, 3, 5, 7, 13, 15, 18, 20, 23, 24, 25, 26, 28, 29, 33, 34, 35, 36, 39, 40, 42, 43, 102

health status, 9, 20, 31, 34, 41, 42
heart, 12
heart attack, 13
hepatitis, 3
HIV, 12
homeland security, x, 101
homicide, 9, 38
hormone, 45
hospice, 23, 26
hospitals, 6, 20, 27, 40, 43, 90
House, viii, 2, 19, 21, 22, 28, 42, 44, 46, 47, 48, 49, 92, 102, 104, 105, 107, 108, 112, 152, 153
House Appropriations Committee, 104
housing, 24, 33, 125
human immunodeficiency virus, 12
human resources, 34, 57

infection, 12
infectious disease(s), 7, 39
inflation, 148, 149, 150, 151
Information System, 49
information technology, 32
infrastructure, 13, 57, 60, 125
injury(ies) 9, 12, 82
innovation, 52
institutions, 33, 108, 117
insulin, 45
insurance, viii, 2, 13, 18, 26, 29
integrity, 61
interest groups, xii, 147, 150, 151
interface, 32
interpretation, x, 60, 89, 96, 114, 154
intervention, x, 33, 111, 113
issue advocacy, xii, 147, 151, 154

I

identification, xii, 8, 44, 78, 140, 143, 145, 148, 152
imaging, 6
immunity, 54, 128, 135
implementation, 33, 73, 75, 78, 104
incidence, viii, 1, 9, 26
income, 31, 66, 149
Indian Child Welfare Act (ICWA), x, 111, 112
Indian Gaming Regulatory Act (IGRA), xi, 121, 122, 134
Indian Health Care Improvement Act (IHCIA), viii, 2, 3, 20
Indian Health Service (IHS), vii, 1, 2, 97, 102
Indian Self-Determination and Education Assistance Act (ISDA), x, 89, 90
indians, vii, viii, xi, 1, 2, 5, 6, 7, 8, 9, 12, 14, 19, 20, 21, 23, 26, 30, 31, 32, 33, 34, 35, 39, 40, 41, 42, 45, 56, 57, 58, 59, 62, 65, 67, 82, 101, 107, 108, 114, 117, 121, 126, 127, 128, 132, 133, 135, 136, 137, 144, 145
indigenous, vii, ix, 72, 73, 75, 83, 84, 85, 107, 108
indigenous peoples, vii, 108
industry, 28

J

judges, 52, 58
judgment, 66, 88
judiciary, 62, 108
Judiciary Committee, 108
jurisdiction, ix, x, 7, 21, 22, 28, 55, 61, 71, 79, 82, 101, 111, 113, 114, 115, 117, 118, 128, 136, 137, 146

K

Kennewick Man, ix, x, 71, 72, 73, 79, 80, 81, 82, 83, 85, 86, 88
kidney, 9, 13, 44
kidney failure, 9

L

labor, 148, 149, 150, 152
land, ix, x, xi, 7, 31, 35, 40, 51, 52, 53, 56, 58, 59, 60, 61, 67, 71, 73, 74, 75, 76, 79, 101, 105, 106, 113, 114, 121, 122, 123, 124, 125, 126, 127, 128, 131, 132, 133, 134, 135, 136, 137, 140, 144, 145
land acquisition, x, 101, 123, 125

land use, 125
language, 19, 22, 26, 29, 38, 53, 55, 65, 84, 91, 93, 94, 96, 97, 115, 122, 125, 134, 140
laws, vii, ix, 29, 51, 52, 62, 69, 84, 106, 112, 118, 145
lead, viii, 2, 56, 57
legal issues, ix, 51, 52
legality, 60
legislation, vii, 21, 39, 45, 73, 78, 84, 91, 92, 93, 102, 104, 107, 112, 125, 128, 139, 140, 143, 145
legislative proposals, 117
licenses, 30
life expectancy, viii, 1, 9
lifestyle, 13, 31
lifestyle changes, 13
likelihood, 140
limitation, 23, 106, 126
links, 140
literature, 64
litigation, ix, 51, 52, 62, 73, 79, 80, 81, 82, 86, 104, 133, 136, 138, 145
loans, 27, 32
local community, xi, 106, 121, 124, 125, 144
local government, 28, 36, 41, 107, 125, 143
location, 7, 74
logging, 74, 76

medical care, 39, 40, 46
Medicare, viii, 2, 13, 14, 17, 18, 20, 21, 23, 26, 28, 29, 34, 36, 41, 47, 48, 102
medication, 13
medicine, 24, 40
membership, vii, 7, 8, 44, 112, 127, 140, 143, 145
membership criteria, 7, 44, 140, 145
memory, 42
mental health, 3, 23, 26, 33, 38, 39, 102
Mexico, 31, 59, 60
military, 39, 40, 46
Millennium, 43, 46
mining, 76
Mississippi, 114
Missouri, x, 63, 72
modernization, 27
money, vii, xii, 60, 92, 93, 94, 97, 104, 133, 147, 148, 150, 152
Montana, 61, 62, 68, 137
moratorium, 61, 68, 91, 93
morbidity, 9, 39
mortality, viii, 1, 9, 12
mortality rate, 9, 12
motion, 87, 108
mountains, 133
movement, 8, 90

M

Maintenance, 16
males, 12
management, x, 19, 20, 23, 32, 37, 68, 90, 91, 95, 101, 103, 105
mandates, 33
mapping, 104
market, 60, 135, 136
marketability, 123
marketing, 60, 68
marriage, 140
meanings, 122
measures, 9, 13, 26
Medicaid, viii, 2, 13, 14, 17, 18, 20, 21, 23, 26, 28, 29, 30, 31, 34, 35, 36, 41, 46, 47, 48, 102

N

nation, 2, 117, 137
National Institutes of Health (NIH), 13, 15, 45
National Labor Relations Act, 36
National Park Service, 85, 86, 87
national parks, 53
national parties, 150, 153
Native American(s), vii, ix, x, 21, 45, 71, 72, 73, 74, 75, 76, 77, 78, 79, 80, 81, 82, 83, 84, 85, 86, 88, 101, 109, 112
Native American Graves Protection and Repatriation Act (NAGPRA), ix, 71
Native Hawaiian, ix, x, 71, 72, 74, 75, 76, 77, 78, 101, 107, 108, 109, 126, 143
natural resources, 57, 60
Nebraska, 41

neglect, 112
negotiating, 20, 52, 63
negotiation, 63
network, 13
New England, 45
New Mexico, 7, 31, 59, 60
New York, vi, xi, 41, 127, 131, 132, 133, 134, 136, 137, 145
newspapers, 140
Newton, 117
North America, vii, 45, 140
nurses, 6
nursing, 24

O

obligation, 3, 94, 95, 96, 104
observations, 150
offenders, 68
Oklahoma, x, 3, 7, 30, 38, 44, 48, 49, 89, 90, 97, 98, 99, 124, 127, 128
Omnibus Act, ix, 72, 73, 84
Oneida, vi, xi, 131, 132, 133, 135, 136, 137, 138
oral health, 26
Oregon, 65, 69, 126
organization(s), ix, 3, 6, 20, 23, 27, 31, 32, 34, 36, 37, 39, 41, 43, 71, 72, 74, 75, 76, 77, 78, 91, 93, 122, 123, 148, 150, 154
Ottawa, 144
oversight, x, 72, 76, 85, 104
ownership, 7, 31, 58, 67, 75, 90

P

PACs, xii, 147, 148, 149, 150, 151
parents, x, 111, 112, 113, 114, 115, 116
partnership, 148
Pascua Yaqui Tribe of Arizona, 44
patient care, 13
penalties, 74, 78
per capita expenditure, 15
performance, 13
permit, 41, 74, 83, 122, 124

personal, 5, 10, 18, 32, 47
personal communication, 5, 10, 47
pharmacists, 6
planning, viii, 37, 51, 52, 57, 90
political action committee, xii, 147, 149
political parties, xii, 148, 149, 150, 153
poor, 9
population, viii, 1, 2, 7, 8, 9, 10, 12, 18, 20, 25, 27, 31, 34, 38, 41, 46, 51, 52, 54, 57, 64, 80, 81
population size, 27
power, vii, 54, 55, 63, 65, 68, 107, 122, 123, 127, 128, 132
preference, 28, 114, 116
pregnancy, 7
premiums, 23, 30
pressure, viii, 51
prevention, 3, 13, 23, 25, 26, 32, 33, 39
price index, 45
production, 78, 104
professions, 18, 20
profit, 73, 152
program, vii, viii, 1, 2, 3, 13, 14, 15, 18, 19, 20, 23, 24, 25, 28, 29, 32, 33, 34, 35, 37, 38, 39, 46, 92, 107
promote, 13, 112
property taxes, 133, 138
prostate cancer, 12
public domain, 53
public health, 21
public interest, 28

R

race, 8, 10, 12, 44, 107, 108
racial groups, 39
radio, 152
radius, 125
range, vii, 7, 8, 23, 26, 36
reading, 154
reasoning, 58
recognition, x, xi, 7, 44, 101, 107, 108, 112, 121, 124, 125, 126, 127, 128, 132, 139, 140, 142, 143, 144
reduction, 6, 91, 93, 94, 96

reforms, 103
regional, vii, 1, 3, 7, 105
regulation(s), x, xi, 6, 28, 29, 32, 33, 34, 35, 40, 41, 61, 62, 68, 73, 79, 86, 101, 121, 124, 125, 134, 138, 140, 150, 153
relationship(s), 53, 61, 76, 78, 79, 80, 81, 82, 90, 107, 113, 125, 128, 132, 144
repair, 102
reservation, ix, xi, 2, 31, 33, 51, 52, 53, 54, 55, 56, 57, 58, 59, 60, 61, 62, 64, 106, 113, 114, 121, 122, 123, 124, 127, 128, 131, 132, 133, 134, 136, 137, 144
reserves, ix, 51, 52, 53
resolution, ix, 71, 72, 78, 87, 90, 116, 145
resources, 6, 18, 35, 42, 60, 61, 97, 126, 145
responsiveness, 143
restructuring, 57
retention, 24, 102, 103
retinopathy, 13
returns, 56
Rhode Island, 128
risk, 13, 38, 83, 95
rural communities, 25
rust, 103

S

safe drinking water, 6
sales, 58, 133
sample, 86, 87
sampling, 104
sanitation, 4, 6, 18, 19, 27, 28, 35, 41
savings, 78
SCHIP, 15, 21, 23, 26, 28, 29, 30, 31, 36, 37, 47, 48, 102
school, 24, 26, 40, 140
science, 79, 80
scientific community, 79, 80, 83
search, 55, 73, 143
security, 46, 112
self-government, vii
Senate, viii, x, 2, 19, 21, 22, 28, 38, 39, 43, 46, 47, 48, 49, 72, 73, 85, 88, 92, 102, 105, 107, 108, 152, 153

Senate Finance Committee, viii, 2, 21, 22, 28, 102
sensitivity, 57
separation, x, 111, 112
series, ix, 48, 71
settlements, ix, 51, 52, 55, 57, 63, 106, 125, 126
severity, 40
sewage, 6
shares, 21, 83, 92
sharing, 29
shoulders, 54
skeleton, 80, 81
skills, 24
smallpox, 39, 40
social environment, 23
social problems, 38
Social Security, viii, 2, 21, 22, 36, 102
social services, 23
social structure, 125
social workers, 112
soft money, xii, 147, 148, 150, 151
SOI, xi, 121, 123, 124, 125, 126, 127, 128
soil, 56
solid waste, 6
South Carolina, 3
South Dakota, 26, 127
sovereignty, xi, 61, 68, 107, 108, 131, 132, 136
specificity, xi, 121, 125
spectrum, 57
speculation, 138
stability, 112
staffing, 26, 103
stages, 103
standards, xi, 25, 28, 29, 31, 54, 56, 104, 121, 124, 144
State Children's Health Insurance Program, 15
state control, 107
state laws, 112
statistics, 9
statutes, 2, 18, 19, 93, 122, 123
stock, 6, 59
stress, 53

strictures, 138
stroke, 13
students, 39
subsistence, 31
substance abuse, 20, 23, 32, 33, 38, 39
substitutes, 33
sugar, 13, 45
suicide, 9, 33, 38
summaries, 75, 87
summer, x, 72
supervision, 54
supervisor(s), 40, 141
suppliers, 32
supply, 6, 56, 63, 141
Supreme Court, x, xi, 3, 38, 53, 54, 55, 56, 57, 58, 59, 60, 61, 62, 63, 64, 66, 83, 89, 90, 92, 94, 95, 96, 114, 131, 132, 133, 135, 136, 137, 145, 153
surplus, 58, 67
survival, 112
systems, 6, 27, 55, 103

T

taxation, x, xi, 101, 128, 131, 132, 133, 134, 135, 136, 137
technical assistance, 6, 27, 141
technology, 57
teenagers, 79
television, 152
tension, 34, 93
territory, 54, 107, 132
Texas, 7, 69
theory, 60
therapists, 25
threshold, 26, 59, 60
timber, 59
time, xi, xii, 6, 19, 21, 25, 34, 37, 40, 44, 53, 55, 63, 64, 76, 79, 85, 86, 87, 114, 115, 116, 124, 125, 128, 131, 132, 135, 139, 141, 145
time frame, 55, 141
Title III, 27, 37, 69
tongue, 63
tracking, 21

traditional practices, 24
training, 13, 24, 25, 32, 37
training programs, 24
transactions, 104
transition, 63, 64
transparency, 125
treaties, 2, 35, 40, 133
treatment programs, 20, 23, 39
tribal lands, ix, xi, 71, 72, 74, 75, 76, 126, 131, 134, 136, 137
tribal rights, ix, 51, 52
trust, x, xi, 2, 7, 30, 35, 53, 54, 58, 60, 61, 67, 97, 101, 103, 104, 105, 106, 121, 122, 123, 124, 125, 126, 127, 128, 136, 140, 144
trust fund, x, 101, 103
tuberculosis, 9, 12, 40

U

uncertainty, 57, 83
unemployment, 37
unions, xii, 148, 149, 150, 152
United States, vii, ix, x, 4, 25, 38, 39, 41, 42, 53, 54, 55, 57, 58, 59, 61, 64, 65, 66, 67, 68, 69, 72, 73, 74, 75, 77, 79, 80, 81, 84, 85, 87, 90, 92, 98, 103, 107, 108, 122, 126, 127, 132, 136, 143, 144, 145
urban areas, vii, 1, 2, 8
users, 18, 53

V

vaccinations, 40
vaccine, 40
validity, 133, 137, 140
values, 103, 112
vandalism, x, 72
victims, 26
village, 5, 117, 134
Virginia, 127, 144

W

war, vii, 113

warrants, 80, 81
Washington, 11, 41, 42, 43, 44, 45, 46, 47, 48, 49, 79, 88
waste disposal, 6
water rights, ix, 51, 52, 53, 54, 55, 56, 57, 58, 60, 61, 63, 64, 65, 67
websites, 109
welfare, x, 61, 101
welfare reform, x, 101
wildlife, 59, 126
Winters doctrine, ix, 51, 52, 53, 62

Wisconsin, 40, 128
witnesses, 78, 85
work environment, 23
writing, 22, 74, 76, 115

young adults, 9